VIRGINIA STATE PARKS BUCKET JOURNAL

Visit the State Parks, Wilderness Areas and Historic Districts of Virginia, USA

This book belongs to

_____

If found please call

_____

"**I only went out** for a walk, and finally concluded to stay out till sundown, for going out, I found, was really going in." ~John Muir

"**A lot of good things start in Virginia**; a lot of good things have started in Virginia. We're no strangers to firsts." ~Robert Hurt

"**Certainly a wilderness area**, a little portion of our planet left alone… will furnish us with a number of very important uses… If we are wise, we will cherish what we have left of such places in our land" ~ Olaus Murie

VIRGINIA STATE PARKS BUCKET JOURNAL

©2021 by My Bucket Journals LLC
Hutto, Texas 78634

Designed and printed in the USA. All rights reserved.

This publication may not be reproduced stored or transmitted in whole or in part, in any form or by any means, electronic, mechanical or otherwise, without prior written consent from the publisher and author.

Brief quotations may be included in a review. If in PDF form, it may be stored on your computer and you may keep one online digital copy. This publication may be printed for personal use only.

Disclaimer
The information in this book is based on the author's opinion, knowledge and experience. The publisher and the author will not be held liable for the use or misuse of the information contained herein.

Disclosure
This book may contain affiliate links. If you click through an affiliate link to a third-party website and make a purchase, the author may receive a small commission.

Cover photo ©DepositPhotos

The State of Virginia is a diverse state of rounded mountain ranges, and lush valleys with rolling hills, caves, caverns, and hot springs. The coastal plain has abounding opportunity for exploration.

Some of the parks in this journal are well known and some are less traveled, all are waiting for you to discover their unique qualities.

In this Virginia State Parks Bucket Journal, **you will find individual pages for 93 state parks, wilderness areas, and historic districts** in the beautiful State of Virginia. Many allow for overnight camping and all are great for day use trips.

This bucket journal is different. It gives you the ability to create your own unique exploration of whichever state park or historic site you choose

How to Use Your Virginia State Parks Bucket Journal

Parks that offer camping or other accommodations are on green pages.
- Search out details about the state park or recreational site by using the website URL provided.
- Have fun planning the things you want to see on the left side of the 2-page spread. This is best done before you take your trip, but can be done while you are out exploring.
- On the right side, chronicle everything that you do and experience. Included is space for journaling and reflection about your stay in the park.

Parks that are Day Use Area Only are on blue pages.
- Day use parks are still fun to visit, even if you can't sleep there.
- Visit them when you are staying at other overnight parks or use them as day trip excursions to get out and explore.

Historic Districts are on teal pages.
- Plenty of room for planning your next shopping adventure
- Records the historic sites you visit
- Plan the museums you want to visit
- Note your favorite restaurants and eateries

The Virginia State Parks Bucket Journal will become a living memory for your trips and adventures as you discover the wonders around you.

Enjoy exploring the beauty that is Virginia!

TABLE OF CONTENTS

- State Map...................6

Central Region...................7

Overnight Parks
- Holliday Lake State Park...................8
- Smith Mountain Lake State Park...10
- Pocahontas State Park...................12
- Bear Creek Lake State Park...........14
- Staunton River State Park.............16
- Occoneechee State Park................18
- James River State Park.................20
- Powhatan State Park.....................22
- Twin Lakes State Park...................24
- Lake Anna State Park....................26

Day Use Parks
- Staunton River Battlefield SP.........28
- Shenandoah Wilderness.................29
- The Priest Wilderness....................30
- Three Ridges Wilderness................31
- High Bridge Trail State Park...........32
- Sailor's Creek Battlefield HSP........33

Historic District
- University Of Virginia HD...............34
- Lynchburg Historic District.............36
- Charlotte Court House HD.............38
- Bremo Historic District..................40
- South Boston HD..........................42
- Jackson Ward Historic District.......44
- Monument Avenue HD...................46
- Martinsville Historic District..........48
- Green Springs Historic District......50
- Clarksville Historic District & Walking Tour...................52
- Historic Blackstone.......................54
- Spotsylvania Historic District.........56

Eastern Shore Region...........59

Overnight Parks
- Kiptopeke State Park......................60

Historic District
- Accomac Historic District...............62

Northern Region...................65

Overnight Parks
- Sky Meadows State Park................66
- Leeslvania State Park....................68

Day Use Parks
- Mason Neck State Park..................70
- Widewater State Park....................71

Historic District
- Fort Myer Historic District.............72
- Alexandria Historic District.............74
- Potomac Canal Historic District.....76
- Historic Herndon...........................78
- Virginia Piedmont HA....................80
- Leesburg Historic District..............82
- Waterford Historic District.............84

Shenandoah Valley Region...87

Overnight Parks
- Douthat State Park........................88
- Barbours Creek Wilderness............90
- Shawvers Run Wilderness..............92
- Cave Mountain Lake Rec. Area......94

Day Use Parks
- Ramsey's Draft Wilderness............96
- Rough Mountain Wilderness..........97
- Rich Hole Wilderness.....................98
- Thunder Ridge Wilderness.............99
- St. Mary's Wilderness...................100
- Natural Bridge State Park.............101
- James River Face Wilderness.......102
- Seven Bends State Park................103

HA: Heritage Area *HD: Historic District/Downtown* *HSP: Historic State Park* *SP: State Park*

TABLE OF CONTENTS

Shenandoah Valley cont.

Historic District
- ☐ Historic Downtown Staunton......104
- ☐ Historic Buchanan.........................106
- ☐ Skyline Drive Historic District......108
- ☐ Virginia Military Institute HD......110
- ☐ Historic New Market...................112
- ☐ Shenandoah Valley Battlefields National Historic District..............114
- ☐ Thunderbird Archaeological District...116

Southwestern Region.........119

Overnight Parks
- ☐ Breaks Interstate State Park........120
- ☐ Grayson Highlands State Park......122
- ☐ Lewis Fork Wilderness.................124
- ☐ Wilderness Road State Park........126
- ☐ Fairy Stone State Park.................128
- ☐ Claytor Lake State Park................130
- ☐ Natural Tunnel State Park...........132
- ☐ Hungry Mother State Park..........134
- ☐ Raccoon Branch Wilderness.......136
- ☐ Little Wilson Creek Wilderness..138
- ☐ Southwest Virginia Museum Historical State Park.....................140
- ☐ New River Trail State Park...........142

Day Use Parks
- ☐ Kimberling Creek Wilderness......144
- ☐ Mountain Lake Wilderness..........145
- ☐ Peters Mountain Wilderness.......146
- ☐ Stone Mountain Wilderness.......147
- ☐ Brush Mountain Wilderness.......148
- ☐ Brush Mountain East Wilderness.................................149
- ☐ Garden Mountain Wilderness....150

Southwestern Region cont.

- ☐ Beartown Wilderness..................151
- ☐ Hunting Camp Creek Wilderness..................................152
- ☐ Shot Tower State Park.................153
- ☐ Little Dry Run Wilderness..........154

Historic District
- ☐ Historic Saltville..........................156
- ☐ Abingdon Historic District..........158

Tidewater Region.................161

Overnight Parks
- ☐ Caledon State Park......................162
- ☐ Belle Isle State Park....................164
- ☐ Chippokes Plantation SP..............166
- ☐ False Cape State Park..................168
- ☐ First Landing State Park..............170
- ☐ Westmoreland State Park...........172

Day Use Parks
- ☐ York River State Park...................174

Historic District
- ☐ Historic Jamestown.....................176

Add More Overnight Parks

- ☐ _____178
- ☐ _____180
- ☐ _____182

Add More Day Parks

- ☐ _____184
- ☐ _____185
- ☐ _____186
- ☐ _____187

Add More Historic Districts

- ☐ _____188
- ☐ _____190
- ☐ _____192

HD: *Historic District/Downtown* HSP: *Historic State Park* SP: *State Park*

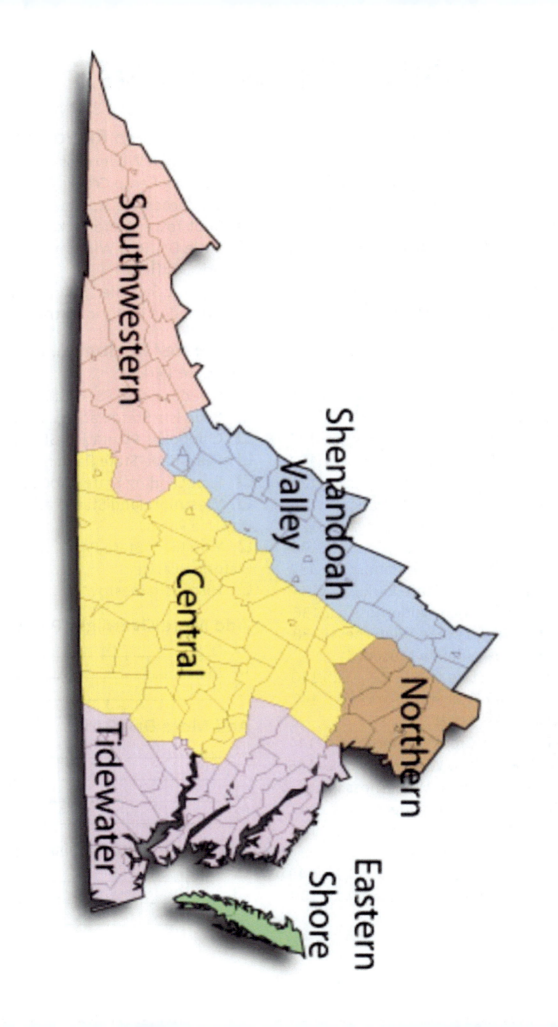

Holliday Lake State Park
City: Appomattox   County: Appomattox

Plan your trip: https://www.dcr.virginia.gov/state-parks/holliday-lake

Activities:

- ☐ Appalachian Trail
- ☐ Archery
- ☐ Biking
- ☐ Boating
- ☐ Camping
- ☐ Fishing
- ☐ Hiking
- ☐ Historic Sites
- ☐ Horseback Riding
- ☐ Hunting
- ☐ Photography
- ☐ Swimming
- ☐ Wildlife & Birding
- ☐
- ☐
- ☐
- ☐
- ☐
- ☐
- ☐
- ☐
- ☐
- ☐
- ☐
- ☐
- ☐
- ☐
- ☐
- ☐
- ☐
- ☐
- ☐
- ☐
- ☐
- ☐

Facilities:

- ☐ ADA
- ☐ Picnic sites
- ☐ Restrooms / Showers
- ☐ Trailer Access
- ☐ Visitor center
- ☐ Group Camping
- ☐ RV Camp
- ☐ Rustic Camping
- ☐ Cabins / Yurts / Bunkhouses
- ☐ Day Use Area

Notes:

Get the Facts

- ☐ Phone   434-248-6308
- ☐ Park Hours

  _____
- ☐ Reservations? ____Y ____N

  date made_____
- ☐ Open all year ____Y____N

  dates_____
- ☐ Check in time _____
- ☐ Check out time _____
- ☐ Pet friendly _____Y _____N
- ☐ Max RV length _____
- ☐ Distance from home

  miles: _____

  hours: _____
- ☐ Address_____

  _____

  _____

Fees:

- ☐ Day Use $ _____
- ☐ Camp Sites $ _____
- ☐ RV Sites $ _____
- ☐ Refund policy

  _____

  _____

  _____

Make It Personal

Trip dates: _____ | The weather was: Sunny Cloudy Rainy Stormy Snowy Foggy Warm Cold

Why I went:
_____

How I got there: (circle all that apply)   Plane   Train   Car   Bus   Bike   Hike   RV   MC

I went with:
_____

We stayed in (space, cabin # etc):
_____

Most relaxing day:
_____

Something funny:
_____

Someone we met:
_____

Best story told:
_____

The kids liked this:
_____

The best food:
_____

Games played:
_____

Something disappointing:
_____

Next time I'll do this differently:
_____

Smith Mountain Lake State Park
City: Huddleston   County: Bedford

Plan your trip: https://www.dcr.virginia.gov/state-parks/smith-mountain-lake

Activities:

- ❑ Appalachian Trail
- ❑ Archery
- ❑ Biking
- ❑ Boating
- ❑ Camping
- ❑ Fishing
- ❑ Hiking
- ❑ Historic Sites
- ❑ Horseback Riding
- ❑ Hunting
- ❑ Photography
- ❑ Swimming

- ❑ Wildlife & Birding
- ❑
- ❑
- ❑
- ❑
- ❑
- ❑
- ❑
- ❑
- ❑
- ❑

- ❑
- ❑
- ❑
- ❑
- ❑
- ❑
- ❑
- ❑
- ❑
- ❑
- ❑

Facilities:

- ❑ ADA
- ❑ Picnic sites
- ❑ Restrooms / Showers
- ❑ Trailer Access
- ❑ Visitor center
- ❑ Group Camping
- ❑ RV Camp
- ❑ Rustic Camping
- ❑ Cabins / Yurts / Bunkhouses
- ❑ Day Use Area

Notes:

Get the Facts

- ❑ Phone   540-297-6066
- ❑ Park Hours

  _____

- ❑ Reservations? ____Y ____N

  date made_____

- ❑ Open all year ____Y____N

  dates_____

- ❑ Check in time _____
- ❑ Check out time _____
- ❑ Pet friendly _____Y _____N
- ❑ Max RV length _____
- ❑ Distance from home

  miles: _____

  hours: _____

- ❑ Address_____

  _____

  _____

Fees:

- ❑ Day Use $ _____
- ❑ Camp Sites $ _____
- ❑ RV Sites $ _____
- ❑ Refund policy

  _____

  _____

  _____

Make It Personal

Trip dates: _____ | The weather was: Sunny   Cloudy   Rainy   Stormy   Snowy   Foggy   Warm   Cold

Why I went:
_____

How I got there: (circle all that apply)   Plane   Train   Car   Bus   Bike   Hike   RV   MC

I went with:
_____

We stayed in (space, cabin # etc):
_____

Most relaxing day:
_____

Something funny:
_____

Someone we met:
_____

Best story told:
_____

The kids liked this:
_____

The best food:
_____

Games played:
_____

Something disappointing:
_____

Next time I'll do this differently:
_____

Pocahontas State Park
City: Chesterfield   County: Chesterfield

Plan your trip: https://www.dcr.virginia.gov/state-parks/pocahontas

Activities:

- ❑ Appalachian Trail
- ❑ Archery
- ❑ Biking
- ❑ Boating
- ❑ Camping
- ❑ Fishing
- ❑ Hiking
- ❑ Historic Sites
- ❑ Horseback Riding
- ❑ Hunting
- ❑ Photography
- ❑ Swimming

- ❑ Wildlife & Birding
- ❑
- ❑
- ❑
- ❑
- ❑
- ❑
- ❑
- ❑
- ❑

- ❑
- ❑
- ❑
- ❑
- ❑
- ❑
- ❑
- ❑
- ❑
- ❑
- ❑
- ❑

Facilities:

- ❑ ADA
- ❑ Picnic sites
- ❑ Restrooms / Showers
- ❑ Trailer Access
- ❑ Visitor center
- ❑ Group Camping
- ❑ RV Camp
- ❑ Rustic Camping
- ❑ Cabins / Yurts / Bunkhouses
- ❑ Day Use Area

Notes:

Get the Facts

- ❑ Phone   804-796-4255
- ❑ Park Hours

  _____

- ❑ Reservations? _____Y _____N

  date made_____

- ❑ Open all year _____Y_____N

  dates_____

- ❑ Check in time _____
- ❑ Check out time _____
- ❑ Pet friendly _____Y _____N
- ❑ Max RV length _____
- ❑ Distance from home

  miles: _____

  hours: _____

- ❑ Address_____

  _____

  _____

Fees:

- ❑ Day Use $ _____
- ❑ Camp Sites $ _____
- ❑ RV Sites $ _____
- ❑ Refund policy

  _____

  _____

  _____

Make It Personal

Trip dates: _____ | The weather was: Sunny Cloudy Rainy Stormy Snowy Foggy Warm Cold

Why I went:
_____

How I got there: (circle all that apply) Plane Train Car Bus Bike Hike RV MC

I went with:
_____

We stayed in (space, cabin # etc):
_____

Most relaxing day:
_____

Something funny:
_____

Someone we met:
_____

Best story told:
_____

The kids liked this:
_____

The best food:
_____

Games played:
_____

Something disappointing:
_____

Next time I'll do this differently:
_____

Bear Creek Lake State Park
City: Cumberland   County: Cumberland

Plan your trip: https://www.dcr.virginia.gov/state-parks/bear-creek-lake

Activities:

- ❑ Appalachian Trail
- ❑ Archery
- ❑ Biking
- ❑ Boating
- ❑ Camping
- ❑ Fishing
- ❑ Hiking
- ❑ Historic Sites
- ❑ Horseback Riding
- ❑ Hunting
- ❑ Photography
- ❑ Swimming
- ❑ Wildlife & Birding
- ❑
- ❑
- ❑
- ❑
- ❑
- ❑
- ❑
- ❑
- ❑
- ❑

Facilities:

- ❑ ADA
- ❑ Picnic sites
- ❑ Restrooms / Showers
- ❑ Trailer Access
- ❑ Visitor center
- ❑ Group Camping
- ❑ RV Camp
- ❑ Rustic Camping
- ❑ Cabins / Yurts / Bunkhouses
- ❑ Day Use Area

Notes:

Get the Facts

- ❑ Phone   804-492-4410
- ❑ Park Hours

  _____

- ❑ Reservations? ____Y ____N

  date made_____

- ❑ Open all year ____Y____N

  dates_____

- ❑ Check in time _____
- ❑ Check out time _____
- ❑ Pet friendly _____Y _____N
- ❑ Max RV length _____
- ❑ Distance from home

  miles: _____

  hours: _____

- ❑ Address_____

  _____

  _____

Fees:

- ❑ Day Use $ _____
- ❑ Camp Sites $ _____
- ❑ RV Sites $ _____
- ❑ Refund policy

  _____

  _____

  _____

Make It Personal

Trip dates: | The weather was: Sunny Cloudy Rainy Stormy Snowy Foggy Warm Cold

Why I went:

How I got there: (circle all that apply)   Plane   Train   Car   Bus   Bike   Hike   RV   MC

I went with:

We stayed in (space, cabin # etc):

Most relaxing day:

Something funny:

Someone we met:

Best story told:

The kids liked this:

The best food:

Games played:

Something disappointing:

Next time I'll do this differently:

Staunton River State Park
City: Scottsburg   County: Halifax
Plan your trip: https://www.dcr.virginia.gov/state-parks/staunton-river

Activities:

- ❑ Appalachian Trail
- ❑ Archery
- ❑ Biking
- ❑ Boating
- ❑ Camping
- ❑ Fishing
- ❑ Hiking
- ❑ Historic Sites
- ❑ Horseback Riding
- ❑ Hunting
- ❑ Photography
- ❑ Swimming
- ❑ Wildlife & Birding

Facilities:

- ❑ ADA
- ❑ Picnic sites
- ❑ Restrooms / Showers
- ❑ Trailer Access
- ❑ Visitor center
- ❑ Group Camping
- ❑ RV Camp
- ❑ Rustic Camping
- ❑ Cabins / Yurts / Bunkhouses
- ❑ Day Use Area

Notes:

Get the Facts

- ❑ Phone   434-572-4623
- ❑ Park Hours

  _____

- ❑ Reservations? ____Y ____N

  date made_____

- ❑ Open all year ____Y____N

  dates_____

- ❑ Check in time _____
- ❑ Check out time _____
- ❑ Pet friendly _____Y _____N
- ❑ Max RV length _____
- ❑ Distance from home

  miles: _____

  hours: _____

- ❑ Address_____

  _____

  _____

Fees:

- ❑ Day Use $ _____
- ❑ Camp Sites $ _____
- ❑ RV Sites $ _____
- ❑ Refund policy

  _____

  _____

  _____

Make It Personal

Trip dates: _____ | The weather was: Sunny Cloudy Rainy Stormy Snowy Foggy Warm Cold

Why I went:

_____

How I got there: (circle all that apply)   Plane   Train   Car   Bus   Bike   Hike   RV   MC

I went with:

We stayed in (space, cabin # etc):

Most relaxing day:

_____

Something funny:

_____

Someone we met:

_____

Best story told:

_____

The kids liked this:

_____

The best food:

_____

Games played:

_____

Something disappointing:

_____

Next time I'll do this differently:

_____

Occoneechee State Park
City: Clarksville　　　County: Mecklenburg

Plan your trip: https://www.dcr.virginia.gov/state-parks/occoneechee

Activities:

- ❑ Appalachian Trail
- ❑ Archery
- ❑ Biking
- ❑ Boating
- ❑ Camping
- ❑ Fishing
- ❑ Hiking
- ❑ Historic Sites
- ❑ Horseback Riding
- ❑ Hunting
- ❑ Photography
- ❑ Swimming

- ❑ Wildlife & Birding
- ❑
- ❑
- ❑
- ❑
- ❑
- ❑
- ❑
- ❑
- ❑
- ❑

- ❑
- ❑
- ❑
- ❑
- ❑
- ❑
- ❑
- ❑
- ❑
- ❑
- ❑
- ❑

Facilities:

- ❑ ADA
- ❑ Picnic sites
- ❑ Restrooms / Showers
- ❑ Trailer Access
- ❑ Visitor center
- ❑ Group Camping
- ❑ RV Camp
- ❑ Rustic Camping
- ❑ Cabins / Yurts / Bunkhouses
- ❑ Day Use Area

Notes:

Get the Facts

- ❑ Phone　434-374-2210
- ❑ Park Hours

  _____

- ❑ Reservations? ____Y ____N

  date made_____

- ❑ Open all year ____Y____N

  dates_____

- ❑ Check in time _____
- ❑ Check out time _____
- ❑ Pet friendly _____Y ____N
- ❑ Max RV length _____
- ❑ Distance from home

  miles: _____

  hours: _____

- ❑ Address_____

  _____

  _____

Fees:

- ❑ Day Use $ _____
- ❑ Camp Sites $ _____
- ❑ RV Sites $ _____
- ❑ Refund policy

  _____

  _____

  _____

Make It Personal

Trip dates: _____ | The weather was: Sunny Cloudy Rainy Stormy Snowy Foggy Warm Cold

Why I went:
_____

_____

How I got there: (circle all that apply)   Plane   Train   Car   Bus   Bike   Hike   RV   MC

I went with:
_____

We stayed in (space, cabin # etc):
_____

Most relaxing day:
_____

_____

Something funny:
_____

_____

Someone we met:
_____

_____

Best story told:
_____

_____

The kids liked this:
_____

_____

The best food:
_____

_____

Games played:
_____

_____

Something disappointing:
_____

_____

Next time I'll do this differently:
_____

_____

James River State Park
City: Gladstone   County: Nelson

Plan your trip: https://www.dcr.virginia.gov/state-parks/james-river

Activities:

- ❑ Appalachian Trail
- ❑ Archery
- ❑ Biking
- ❑ Boating
- ❑ Camping
- ❑ Fishing
- ❑ Hiking
- ❑ Historic Sites
- ❑ Horseback Riding
- ❑ Hunting
- ❑ Photography
- ❑ Swimming

- ❑ Wildlife & Birding
- ❑
- ❑
- ❑
- ❑
- ❑
- ❑
- ❑
- ❑
- ❑
- ❑

- ❑
- ❑
- ❑
- ❑
- ❑
- ❑
- ❑
- ❑
- ❑
- ❑
- ❑
- ❑

Facilities:

- ❑ ADA
- ❑ Picnic sites
- ❑ Restrooms / Showers
- ❑ Trailer Access
- ❑ Visitor center
- ❑ Group Camping
- ❑ RV Camp
- ❑ Rustic Camping
- ❑ Cabins / Yurts / Bunkhouses
- ❑ Day Use Area

Notes:

Get the Facts

- ❑ Phone   434-933-4355
- ❑ Park Hours

  _____

- ❑ Reservations? _____Y _____N

  date made_____

- ❑ Open all year _____Y_____N

  dates_____

- ❑ Check in time _____
- ❑ Check out time _____
- ❑ Pet friendly _____Y _____N
- ❑ Max RV length _____
- ❑ Distance from home

  miles: _____

  hours: _____

- ❑ Address_____

  _____

  _____

Fees:

- ❑ Day Use $ _____
- ❑ Camp Sites $ _____
- ❑ RV Sites $ _____
- ❑ Refund policy

  _____

  _____

  _____

Make It Personal

Trip dates: _____ | The weather was: Sunny Cloudy Rainy Stormy Snowy Foggy Warm Cold

Why I went: _____

_____

How I got there: (circle all that apply)   Plane   Train   Car   Bus   Bike   Hike   RV   MC

I went with: _____

We stayed in (space, cabin # etc): _____

Most relaxing day: _____

_____

Something funny: _____

_____

Someone we met: _____

_____

Best story told: _____

_____

The kids liked this: _____

_____

The best food: _____

_____

Games played: _____

_____

Something disappointing: _____

_____

Next time I'll do this differently: _____

_____

Powhatan State Park

City: Powhatan   **County: Powhatan**

Plan your trip: https://www.dcr.virginia.gov/state-parks/powhatan

Activities:

- ❑ Appalachian Trail
- ❑ Archery
- ❑ Biking
- ❑ Boating
- ❑ Camping
- ❑ Fishing
- ❑ Hiking
- ❑ Historic Sites
- ❑ Horseback Riding
- ❑ Hunting
- ❑ Photography
- ❑ Swimming

- ❑ Wildlife & Birding
- ❑
- ❑
- ❑
- ❑
- ❑
- ❑
- ❑
- ❑
- ❑
- ❑

- ❑
- ❑
- ❑
- ❑
- ❑
- ❑
- ❑
- ❑
- ❑
- ❑
- ❑
- ❑

Facilities:

- ❑ ADA
- ❑ Picnic sites
- ❑ Restrooms / Showers
- ❑ Trailer Access
- ❑ Visitor center
- ❑ Group Camping
- ❑ RV Camp
- ❑ Rustic Camping
- ❑ Cabins / Yurts / Bunkhouses
- ❑ Day Use Area

Notes:

Get the Facts

- ❑ Phone   804-598-7148
- ❑ Park Hours

  _____

- ❑ Reservations? ____Y ____N

  date made_____

- ❑ Open all year ____Y____N

  dates_____

- ❑ Check in time _____
- ❑ Check out time _____
- ❑ Pet friendly _____Y _____N
- ❑ Max RV length _____
- ❑ Distance from home

  miles: _____

  hours: _____

- ❑ Address_____

  _____

  _____

Fees:

- ❑ Day Use $ _____
- ❑ Camp Sites $ _____
- ❑ RV Sites $ _____
- ❑ Refund policy

  _____

  _____

  _____

Make It Personal

Trip dates: _____ | The weather was: Sunny Cloudy Rainy Stormy Snowy Foggy Warm Cold

Why I went:
_____

How I got there: (circle all that apply)   Plane   Train   Car   Bus   Bike   Hike   RV   MC

I went with:
_____

We stayed in (space, cabin # etc):
_____

Most relaxing day:
_____

Something funny:
_____

Someone we met:
_____

Best story told:
_____

The kids liked this:
_____

The best food:
_____

Games played:
_____

Something disappointing:
_____

Next time I'll do this differently:
_____

Twin Lakes State Park
City: Green Bay   County: Prince Edward

Plan your trip: https://www.dcr.virginia.gov/state-parks/twin-lakes

Activities:

- ❑ Appalachian Trail
- ❑ Archery
- ❑ Biking
- ❑ Boating
- ❑ Camping
- ❑ Fishing
- ❑ Hiking
- ❑ Historic Sites
- ❑ Horseback Riding
- ❑ Hunting
- ❑ Photography
- ❑ Swimming

- ❑ Wildlife & Birding
- ❑
- ❑
- ❑
- ❑
- ❑
- ❑
- ❑
- ❑
- ❑
- ❑

- ❑
- ❑
- ❑
- ❑
- ❑
- ❑
- ❑
- ❑
- ❑
- ❑
- ❑

Facilities:

- ❑ ADA
- ❑ Picnic sites
- ❑ Restrooms / Showers
- ❑ Trailer Access
- ❑ Visitor center
- ❑ Group Camping
- ❑ RV Camp
- ❑ Rustic Camping
- ❑ Cabins / Yurts / Bunkhouses
- ❑ Day Use Area

Notes:

Get the Facts

- ❑ Phone   434-392-3435
- ❑ Park Hours

_____

- ❑ Reservations? ____Y ____N

date made_____

- ❑ Open all year ____Y_____N

dates_____

- ❑ Check in time _____
- ❑ Check out time _____
- ❑ Pet friendly _____Y _____N
- ❑ Max RV length _____
- ❑ Distance from home

miles: _____

hours: _____

- ❑ Address_____

_____

_____

Fees:

- ❑ Day Use $ _____
- ❑ Camp Sites $ _____
- ❑ RV Sites $ _____
- ❑ Refund policy

_____

_____

_____

Make It Personal

Trip dates: _____ | The weather was: Sunny Cloudy Rainy Stormy Snowy Foggy Warm Cold

Why I went:
_____

How I got there: (circle all that apply) Plane Train Car Bus Bike Hike RV MC

I went with:
_____

We stayed in (space, cabin # etc):
_____

Most relaxing day:
_____

Something funny:
_____

Someone we met:
_____

Best story told:
_____

The kids liked this:
_____

The best food:
_____

Games played:
_____

Something disappointing:
_____

Next time I'll do this differently:
_____

Lake Anna State Park
City: Spotsylvania   County: Spotsylvania
Plan your trip: https://www.dcr.virginia.gov/state-parks/lake-anna

Activities:

- ❑ Appalachian Trail
- ❑ Archery
- ❑ Biking
- ❑ Boating
- ❑ Camping
- ❑ Fishing
- ❑ Hiking
- ❑ Historic Sites
- ❑ Horseback Riding
- ❑ Hunting
- ❑ Photography
- ❑ Swimming

- ❑ Wildlife & Birding
- ❑
- ❑
- ❑
- ❑
- ❑
- ❑
- ❑
- ❑
- ❑
- ❑

- ❑
- ❑
- ❑
- ❑
- ❑
- ❑
- ❑
- ❑
- ❑
- ❑
- ❑
- ❑

Facilities:

- ❑ ADA
- ❑ Picnic sites
- ❑ Restrooms / Showers
- ❑ Trailer Access
- ❑ Visitor center
- ❑ Group Camping
- ❑ RV Camp
- ❑ Rustic Camping
- ❑ Cabins / Yurts / Bunkhouses
- ❑ Day Use Area

Notes:

Get the Facts

- ❑ Phone   540-854-5503
- ❑ Park Hours

  _____

- ❑ Reservations? _____ Y _____ N

  date made_____

- ❑ Open all year _____ Y _____ N

  dates_____

- ❑ Check in time _____
- ❑ Check out time _____
- ❑ Pet friendly _____ Y _____ N
- ❑ Max RV length _____
- ❑ Distance from home

  miles: _____

  hours: _____

- ❑ Address_____

  _____

  _____

Fees:

- ❑ Day Use $ _____
- ❑ Camp Sites $ _____
- ❑ RV Sites $ _____
- ❑ Refund policy

  _____

  _____

  _____

Make It Personal

Trip dates: _____ | The weather was: Sunny Cloudy Rainy Stormy Snowy Foggy Warm Cold

Why I went: _____

How I got there: (circle all that apply) Plane Train Car Bus Bike Hike RV MC

I went with: _____

We stayed in (space, cabin # etc): _____

Most relaxing day: _____

Something funny: _____

Someone we met: _____

Best story told: _____

The kids liked this: _____

The best food: _____

Games played: _____

Something disappointing: _____

Next time I'll do this differently: _____

Staunton River Battlefield State Park
City: Randolph   County: Charlotte

Plan your trip: https://www.dcr.virginia.gov/state-parks/staunton-river-battlefield

Activities:

- ❑ Appalachian Trail   ❑
- ❑ Biking   ❑
- ❑ Boating   ❑
- ❑ Fishing   ❑
- ❑ Hiking   ❑
- ❑ Horseback Riding   ❑
- ❑ Wildlife Viewing   ❑
- ❑ Living History   ❑
- ❑ Re-enactments   ❑
- ❑   ❑
- ❑   ❑

Facilities:

- ❑ ADA   ❑
- ❑ Gift Shop   ❑
- ❑ Museum   ❑
- ❑ Visitor Center   ❑
- ❑ Picnic sites   ❑
- ❑ Restrooms   ❑

Our Visit:

Get the Facts

- ❑ Phone   434-454-4312
- ❑ Park Hours

  _____

- ❑ Reservations? ____Y ____N

  date made_____

- ❑ Open all year? ____Y____N

  dates_____

- ❑ Dog friendly _____Y _____N

- ❑ Distance from home

  miles: _____

  hours: _____

- ❑ Address_____

  _____

  _____

Fees:

- ❑ Day Use $ _____
- ❑ Refund policy

  _____

  _____

  _____

Notes:

Shenandoah Wilderness

City: Syria   County: Madison

Plan your trip: http://www.vawilderness.org/snp-wilderness.html

Activities:

- ☐ Appalachian Trail   ☐
- ☐ Biking   ☐
- ☐ Boating   ☐
- ☐ Fishing   ☐
- ☐ Hiking   ☐
- ☐ Horseback Riding   ☐
- ☐ Wildlife Viewing   ☐
- ☐   ☐
- ☐   ☐
- ☐   ☐
- ☐   ☐

Facilities:

- ☐ ADA   ☐
- ☐ Gift Shop   ☐
- ☐ Museum   ☐
- ☐ Visitor Center   ☐
- ☐ Picnic sites   ☐
- ☐ Restrooms   ☐

Our Visit:

Get the Facts

- ☐ Phone   540-999-3500
- ☐ Park Hours

  _____

- ☐ Reservations? _____Y _____N

  date made_____

- ☐ Open all year? _____Y_____N

  dates_____

- ☐ Dog friendly _____Y _____N

- ☐ Distance from home

  miles: _____

  hours: _____

- ☐ Address_____

  _____

  _____

Fees:

- ☐ Day Use $ _____
- ☐ Refund policy

  _____

  _____

  _____

Notes:

The Priest Wilderness

City: Syria   **County: Madison**

Plan your trip: http://www.vawilderness.org/the-priest-wilderness.html

Activities:

- ☐ Appalachian Trail   ☐
- ☐ Biking   ☐
- ☐ Boating   ☐
- ☐ Fishing   ☐
- ☐ Hiking   ☐
- ☐ Horseback Riding   ☐
- ☐ Wildlife Viewing   ☐
- ☐   ☐
- ☐   ☐
- ☐   ☐
- ☐   ☐

Facilities:

- ☐ ADA   ☐
- ☐ Gift Shop   ☐
- ☐ Museum   ☐
- ☐ Visitor Center   ☐
- ☐ Picnic sites   ☐
- ☐ Restrooms   ☐

Our Visit:

Get the Facts

- ☐ Phone   540-464-1661
- ☐ Park Hours

  _____

- ☐ Reservations? _____Y _____N

  date made_____

- ☐ Open all year? _____Y_____N

  dates_____

- ☐ Dog friendly _____Y _____N

- ☐ Distance from home

  miles: _____

  hours: _____

- ☐ Address_____

  _____

  _____

Fees:

- ☐ Day Use $ _____
- ☐ Refund policy

  _____

  _____

  _____

Notes:

Three Ridges Wilderness
City: Syria   County: Madison

Plan your trip: https://wilderness.net/visit-wilderness/?ID=601

Activities:

- [ ] Appalachian Trail   - [ ]
- [ ] Biking   - [ ]
- [ ] Boating   - [ ]
- [ ] Fishing   - [ ]
- [ ] Hiking   - [ ]
- [ ] Horseback Riding   - [ ]
- [ ] Wildlife Viewing   - [ ]
- [ ]   - [ ]
- [ ]   - [ ]
- [ ]   - [ ]
- [ ]   - [ ]

Facilities:

- [ ] ADA   - [ ]
- [ ] Gift Shop   - [ ]
- [ ] Museum   - [ ]
- [ ] Visitor Center   - [ ]
- [ ] Picnic sites   - [ ]
- [ ] Restrooms   - [ ]

Our Visit:

Get the Facts

- [ ] Phone   540-464-1661
- [ ] Park Hours

  _____

- [ ] Reservations? _____Y _____N

  date made_____

- [ ] Open all year? _____Y_____N

  dates_____

- [ ] Dog friendly _____Y _____N

- [ ] Distance from home

  miles: _____

  hours: _____

- [ ] Address_____

  _____

  _____

Fees:

- [ ] Day Use $ _____
- [ ] Refund policy

  _____

  _____

  _____

Notes:

High Bridge Trail State Park
City: Green Bay   County: Prince Edward

Plan your trip: https://www.dcr.virginia.gov/state-parks/high-bridge-trail

Activities:

- ❑ Appalachian Trail ❑
- ❑ Biking ❑
- ❑ Boating ❑
- ❑ Fishing ❑
- ❑ Hiking ❑
- ❑ Horseback Riding ❑
- ❑ Wildlife Viewing ❑
- ❑ ❑
- ❑ ❑
- ❑ ❑
- ❑ ❑

Facilities:

- ❑ ADA ❑
- ❑ Gift Shop ❑
- ❑ Museum ❑
- ❑ Visitor Center ❑
- ❑ Picnic sites ❑
- ❑ Restrooms ❑

Our Visit:

Get the Facts

- ❑ Phone   434-315-0457
- ❑ Park Hours

_____

- ❑ Reservations? _____Y _____N

date made_____

- ❑ Open all year? _____Y_____N

dates_____

- ❑ Dog friendly _____Y _____N

- ❑ Distance from home

miles: _____

hours: _____

- ❑ Address_____

_____

_____

Fees:

- ❑ Day Use $ _____
- ❑ Refund policy

_____

_____

_____

Notes:

Sailor's Creek Battlefield HSP

City: Rice **County: Prince Edward**

Plan your trip: https://www.dcr.virginia.gov/state-parks/sailors-creek

Activities:

- ☐ Appalachian Trail ☐
- ☐ Biking ☐
- ☐ Boating ☐
- ☐ Fishing ☐
- ☐ Hiking ☐
- ☐ Horseback Riding ☐
- ☐ Wildlife Viewing ☐
- ☐ ☐
- ☐ ☐
- ☐ ☐
- ☐ ☐

Facilities:

- ☐ ADA ☐
- ☐ Gift Shop ☐
- ☐ Museum ☐
- ☐ Visitor Center ☐
- ☐ Picnic sites ☐
- ☐ Restrooms ☐

Our Visit:

Get the Facts

- ☐ Phone   804-561-7510
- ☐ Park Hours

  _____

- ☐ Reservations? _____Y _____N

  date made_____

- ☐ Open all year? _____Y_____N

  dates_____

- ☐ Dog friendly _____Y _____N

- ☐ Distance from home

  miles: _____

  hours: _____

- ☐ Address_____

  _____

  _____

Fees:

- ☐ Day Use $ _____
- ☐ Refund policy

  _____
  _____
  _____

Notes:

University Of Virginia Historic District

City: Charlottesville　　County: Albemarle

Plan your trip: https://www.nps.gov/articles/thomas-jefferson-s-plan-for-the-university-of-virginia-lessons-from-the-lawn-teaching-with-historic-places.htm

History:

Things To Do:

- ❑ ADA availability
- ❑ Public Restrooms
- ❑ Gift Shop
- ❑ Museum
- ❑ Visitor Center
- ❑ Picnic areas
- ❑ Chamber of Commerce

- ❑ Monuments
- ❑ Art Galleries
- ❑ Tours
- ❑ Street Art
- ❑ Natural Areas
- ❑ Living History
- ❑ Cemetery
- ❑ Amphitheater

Places I Want to Visit in the Area:

Restaurants:
Boutiques & Shops:
Monuments:
Museums:

Get the Facts

- ❑ Address_____
  _____
- ❑ Phone 215-597-5814
- ❑ Best season to visit
  _____
- ❑ Pet Friendly　Y　N
- ❑ Reservations?　Y　N
  date made_____
- ❑ Distance from home
  miles: _____
  hours: _____

Budget for this trip:

Parking	$
Food	$
Museums	$
Hotel	$
Shopping	$
Total	$

Notes:

Restaurant:

My Experience:

Shopping:

Best Find:

The shop I want to go back to:

Museum:

The coolest thing I learned about this area:

Other:

Lynchburg Historic Districts
City: Lynchburg   County: Campbell
Plan your trip: https://www.lynchburgvirginia.org/listings/historic-district-walking-tour/

History:

Get the Facts
- ❑ Address_____
- _____
- ❑ Phone   434-847-1811
- ❑ Best season to visit
- _____
- ❑ Pet Friendly   Y   N
- ❑ Reservations?   Y   N
- date made_____
- ❑ Distance from home
- miles: _____
- hours: _____

Things To Do:
- ❑ ADA availability
- ❑ Public Restrooms
- ❑ Gift Shop
- ❑ Museum
- ❑ Visitor Center
- ❑ Picnic areas
- ❑ Chamber of Commerce
- ❑ Monuments
- ❑ Art Galleries
- ❑ Tours
- ❑ Street Art
- ❑ Natural Areas
- ❑ Living History
- ❑ Cemetery
- ❑ Amphitheater

Places I Want to Visit in the Area:

Restaurants:

Boutiques & Shops:

Monuments:

Museums:

Budget for this trip:

Parking	$
Food	$
Museums	$
Hotel	$
Shopping	$
Total	$

Notes:

Restaurant:

My Experience:

Shopping:

Best Find:

The shop I want to go back to:

Museum:

The coolest thing I learned about this area:

Other:

Charlotte Court House Historic District
City: Charlotte Court House   County: Charlotte

Plan your trip: https://www.charlotteva.com/museum/walking_tour.html

History:

Get the Facts

- ❑ Address_____
- _____
- ❑ Phone   434-542-5117
- ❑ Best season to visit
- _____
- ❑ Pet Friendly   Y   N
- ❑ Reservations?   Y   N
- date made_____
- ❑ Distance from home
- miles: _____
- hours: _____

Things To Do:

- ❑ ADA availability
- ❑ Public Restrooms
- ❑ Gift Shop
- ❑ Museum
- ❑ Visitor Center
- ❑ Picnic areas
- ❑ Chamber of Commerce
- ❑ Monuments
- ❑ Art Galleries
- ❑ Tours
- ❑ Street Art
- ❑ Natural Areas
- ❑ Living History
- ❑ Cemetery
- ❑ Amphitheater

Places I Want to Visit in the Area:

Restaurants:

Boutiques & Shops:

Monuments:

Museums:

Budget for this trip:

Parking	$
Food	$
Museums	$
Hotel	$
Shopping	$
Total	$

Notes:

Restaurant:

My Experience:

Shopping:

Best Find:

The shop I want to go back to:

Museum:

The coolest thing I learned about this area:

Other:

Bremo Historic District
City: Bremo Bluff   County: Fluvanna
Plan your trip: http://places.afrovirginia.org/items/show/64?tour=7&index=7

History:

Things To Do:

- ❏ ADA availability
- ❏ Public Restrooms
- ❏ Gift Shop
- ❏ Museum
- ❏ Visitor Center
- ❏ Picnic areas
- ❏ Chamber of Commerce
- ❏ Monuments
- ❏ Art Galleries
- ❏ Tours
- ❏ Street Art
- ❏ Natural Areas
- ❏ Living History
- ❏ Cemetery
- ❏ Amphitheater

Places I Want to Visit in the Area:

Restaurants:
Boutiques & Shops:
Monuments:
Museums:

Get the Facts

- ❏ Address_____
  _____
- ❏ Phone
- ❏ Best season to visit
  _____
- ❏ Pet Friendly   Y   N
- ❏ Reservations?   Y   N
  date made_____
- ❏ Distance from home
  miles: _____
  hours: _____

Budget for this trip:

Parking	$
Food	$
Museums	$
Hotel	$
Shopping	$
Total	$

Notes:

Restaurant:

My Experience:

Shopping:

Best Find:

The shop I want to go back to:

Museum:

The coolest thing I learned about this area:

Other:

South Boston Historic Downtown
City: South Boston   County: Halifax
Plan your trip: http://www.oldhalifax.com/county/SBWalkingTour.htm

History:

Get the Facts

- ❑ Address_____

  _____

- ❑ Phone   434-575-4209
- ❑ Best season to visit

  _____

- ❑ Pet Friendly   Y   N
- ❑ Reservations?   Y   N

  date made_____

- ❑ Distance from home

  miles: _____

  hours: _____

Things To Do:

- ❑ ADA availability
- ❑ Public Restrooms
- ❑ Gift Shop
- ❑ Museum
- ❑ Visitor Center
- ❑ Picnic areas
- ❑ Chamber of Commerce
- ❑ Monuments
- ❑ Art Galleries
- ❑ Tours
- ❑ Street Art
- ❑ Natural Areas
- ❑ Living History
- ❑ Cemetery
- ❑ Amphitheater

Places I Want to Visit in the Area:

Restaurants:

Boutiques & Shops:

Monuments:

Museums:

Budget for this trip:

Parking	$
Food	$
Museums	$
Hotel	$
Shopping	$
Total	$

Notes:

Restaurant:

My Experience:

Shopping:

Best Find:

The shop I want to go back to:

Museum:

The coolest thing I learned about this area:

Other:

Jackson Ward Historic District

City: Richmond   **County: Henrico**

Plan your trip: https://www.hjwa.org/

History:

Things To Do:

- ☐ ADA availability
- ☐ Public Restrooms
- ☐ Gift Shop
- ☐ Museum
- ☐ Visitor Center
- ☐ Picnic areas
- ☐ Chamber of Commerce
- ☐ Monuments
- ☐ Art Galleries
- ☐ Tours
- ☐ Street Art
- ☐ Natural Areas
- ☐ Living History
- ☐ Cemetery
- ☐ Amphitheater

Places I Want to Visit in the Area:

Restaurants:
Boutiques & Shops:
Monuments:
Museums:

Get the Facts

- ☐ Address_____
- _____
- ☐ Phone 804-782-2777
- ☐ Best season to visit
- _____
- ☐ Pet Friendly Y N
- ☐ Reservations? Y N
- date made_____
- ☐ Distance from home
- miles: _____
- hours: _____

Budget for this trip:

Parking	$
Food	$
Museums	$
Hotel	$
Shopping	$
Total	$

Notes:

Restaurant:

My Experience:

Shopping:

Best Find:

The shop I want to go back to:

Museum:

The coolest thing I learned about this area:

Other:

Monument Avenue Historic District
City: Richmond   County: Henrico

Plan your trip:
https://www.livingplaces.com/VA/Independent_Cities/Richmond_City/Monument_Avenue_Historic_District.html

History:

Get the Facts

❑ Address_____

_____

❑ Phone   804-782-2777

❑ Best season to visit

_____

❑ Pet Friendly   Y   N

❑ Reservations?   Y   N

date made_____

❑ Distance from home

miles: _____

hours: _____

Things To Do:

❑ ADA availability
❑ Public Restrooms
❑ Gift Shop
❑ Museum
❑ Visitor Center
❑ Picnic areas
❑ Chamber of Commerce

❑ Monuments
❑ Art Galleries
❑ Tours
❑ Street Art
❑ Natural Areas
❑ Living History
❑ Cemetery
❑ Amphitheater

Places I Want to Visit in the Area:

Restaurants:

Boutiques & Shops:

Monuments:

Museums:

Budget for this trip:

Parking	$
Food	$
Museums	$
Hotel	$
Shopping	$
Total	$

Notes:

Restaurant:

My Experience:

Shopping:

Best Find:

The shop I want to go back to:

Museum:

The coolest thing I learned about this area:

Other:

Martinsville Historic District
City: Martinsville   County: Henry

Plan your trip: http://martinsvilleuptown.net/

History:

Get the Facts

- ❑ Address_____
  _____
- ❑ Phone   276-632-6401
- ❑ Best season to visit
  _____
- ❑ Pet Friendly   Y   N
- ❑ Reservations?   Y   N
  date made_____
- ❑ Distance from home
  miles: _____
  hours: _____

Things To Do:

- ❑ ADA availability
- ❑ Public Restrooms
- ❑ Gift Shop
- ❑ Museum
- ❑ Visitor Center
- ❑ Picnic areas
- ❑ Chamber of Commerce

- ❑ Monuments
- ❑ Art Galleries
- ❑ Tours
- ❑ Street Art
- ❑ Natural Areas
- ❑ Living History
- ❑ Cemetery
- ❑ Amphitheater

Places I Want to Visit in the Area:

Restaurants:

Boutiques & Shops:

Monuments:

Museums:

Budget for this trip:

Parking	$
Food	$
Museums	$
Hotel	$
Shopping	$
Total	$

Notes:

Restaurant:

My Experience:

Shopping:

Best Find:

The shop I want to go back to:

Museum:

The coolest thing I learned about this area:

Other:

Green Springs Historic District
City: Zion Crossroads   County: Louisa

Plan your trip: https://www.louisacounty.com/557/Green-Springs-National-Historic-Landmark

History:

Things To Do:

- ☐ ADA availability
- ☐ Public Restrooms
- ☐ Gift Shop
- ☐ Museum
- ☐ Visitor Center
- ☐ Picnic areas
- ☐ Chamber of Commerce
- ☐ Monuments
- ☐ Art Galleries
- ☐ Tours
- ☐ Street Art
- ☐ Natural Areas
- ☐ Living History
- ☐ Cemetery
- ☐ Amphitheater

Places I Want to Visit in the Area:

Restaurants:

Boutiques & Shops:

Monuments:

Museums:

Get the Facts

- ☐ Address_____
- _____
- ☐ Phone   540-967-0401
- ☐ Best season to visit
- _____
- ☐ Pet Friendly   Y   N
- ☐ Reservations?   Y   N
- date made_____
- ☐ Distance from home
- miles: _____
- hours: _____

Budget for this trip:

Parking	$
Food	$
Museums	$
Hotel	$
Shopping	$
Total	$

Notes:

Restaurant:

My Experience:

Shopping:

Best Find:

The shop I want to go back to:

Museum:

The coolest thing I learned about this area:

Other:

Clarksville Historic District & Walking Tour
City: Clarksville County: Mecklenburg

Plan your trip: https://clarksvilleva.com/clarksville/historical-sites/

History:

Things To Do:

- ☐ ADA availability
- ☐ Public Restrooms
- ☐ Gift Shop
- ☐ Museum
- ☐ Visitor Center
- ☐ Picnic areas
- ☐ Chamber of Commerce

- ☐ Monuments
- ☐ Art Galleries
- ☐ Tours
- ☐ Street Art
- ☐ Natural Areas
- ☐ Living History
- ☐ Cemetery
- ☐ Amphitheater

Get the Facts

- ☐ Address_____

  _____

- ☐ Phone   434-374-2436
- ☐ Best season to visit

  _____

- ☐ Pet Friendly   Y   N
- ☐ Reservations?   Y   N

  date made_____

- ☐ Distance from home

  miles: _____

  hours: _____

Budget for this trip:

Parking	$
Food	$
Museums	$
Hotel	$
Shopping	$
Total	$

Places I Want to Visit in the Area:

Restaurants:

Boutiques & Shops:

Monuments:

Museums:

Notes:

Restaurant:

My Experience:

Shopping:

Best Find:

The shop I want to go back to:

Museum:

The coolest thing I learned about this area:

Other:

Historic Blackstone
City: Blackstone   County: Nottoway

Plan your trip: https://www.virginia.org/listings/HistoricSites/AWalkingTourofHistoricBlackstone/

History:

Things To Do:

- ❑ ADA availability
- ❑ Public Restrooms
- ❑ Gift Shop
- ❑ Museum
- ❑ Visitor Center
- ❑ Picnic areas
- ❑ Chamber of Commerce
- ❑ Monuments
- ❑ Art Galleries
- ❑ Tours
- ❑ Street Art
- ❑ Natural Areas
- ❑ Living History
- ❑ Cemetery
- ❑ Amphitheater

Places I Want to Visit in the Area:

Restaurants:
Boutiques & Shops:
Monuments:
Museums:

Get the Facts

- ❑ Address_____
  _____
- ❑ Phone   434-292-677
- ❑ Best season to visit
  _____
- ❑ Pet Friendly   Y   N
- ❑ Reservations?   Y   N
  date made_____
- ❑ Distance from home
  miles: _____
  hours: _____

Budget for this trip:

Parking	$
Food	$
Museums	$
Hotel	$
Shopping	$
Total	$

Notes:

Restaurant:

My Experience:

Shopping:

Best Find:

The shop I want to go back to:

Museum:

The coolest thing I learned about this area:

Other:

Spotsylvania Historic District
City: Spotsylvania   County: Spotsylvania

Plan your trip: https://www.spotsylvania.va.us/101/Visitors

History:

Things To Do:

- ❑ ADA availability
- ❑ Public Restrooms
- ❑ Gift Shop
- ❑ Museum
- ❑ Visitor Center
- ❑ Picnic areas
- ❑ Chamber of Commerce
- ❑ Monuments
- ❑ Art Galleries
- ❑ Tours
- ❑ Street Art
- ❑ Natural Areas
- ❑ Living History
- ❑ Cemetery
- ❑ Amphitheater

Places I Want to Visit in the Area:

Restaurants:

Boutiques & Shops:

Monuments:

Museums:

Get the Facts

- ❑ Address_____
  _____
- ❑ Phone   540-507-7090
- ❑ Best season to visit
  _____
- ❑ Pet Friendly   Y   N
- ❑ Reservations?   Y   N
  date made_____
- ❑ Distance from home
  miles: _____
  hours: _____

Budget for this trip:

Parking	$
Food	$
Museums	$
Hotel	$
Shopping	$
Total	$

Notes:

Restaurant:

My Experience:

Shopping:

Best Find:

The shop I want to go back to:

Museum:

The coolest thing I learned about this area:

Other:

Notes:

Kiptopeke State Park
City: Cape Charles   County: Northampton

Plan your trip: https://www.dcr.virginia.gov/state-parks/kiptopeke

Activities:

- ❏ Appalachian Trail
- ❏ Archery
- ❏ Biking
- ❏ Boating
- ❏ Camping
- ❏ Fishing
- ❏ Hiking
- ❏ Historic Sites
- ❏ Horseback Riding
- ❏ Hunting
- ❏ Photography
- ❏ Swimming

- ❏ Wildlife & Birding
- ❏
- ❏
- ❏
- ❏
- ❏
- ❏
- ❏
- ❏
- ❏

- ❏
- ❏
- ❏
- ❏
- ❏
- ❏
- ❏
- ❏
- ❏
- ❏
- ❏
- ❏

Facilities:

- ❏ ADA
- ❏ Picnic sites
- ❏ Restrooms / Showers
- ❏ Trailer Access
- ❏ Visitor center
- ❏ Group Camping
- ❏ RV Camp
- ❏ Rustic Camping
- ❏ Cabins / Yurts / Bunkhouses
- ❏ Day Use Area

Notes:

Get the Facts

- ❏ Phone   757-331-2267
- ❏ Park Hours

  _____

- ❏ Reservations? ____Y ____N

  date made_____

- ❏ Open all year ____Y_____N

  dates_____

- ❏ Check in time _____
- ❏ Check out time _____
- ❏ Pet friendly _____Y ـــــN
- ❏ Max RV length _____
- ❏ Distance from home

  miles: _____

  hours: _____

- ❏ Address_____

  _____

  _____

Fees:

- ❏ Day Use $ _____
- ❏ Camp Sites $ _____
- ❏ RV Sites $ _____
- ❏ Refund policy

  _____

  _____

  _____

Make It Personal

Trip dates: _____ | The weather was: Sunny Cloudy Rainy Stormy Snowy Foggy Warm Cold

Why I went:
_____

How I got there: (circle all that apply)   Plane   Train   Car   Bus   Bike   Hike   RV   MC

I went with:
_____

We stayed in (space, cabin # etc):
_____

Most relaxing day:
_____

Something funny:
_____

Someone we met:
_____

Best story told:
_____

The kids liked this:
_____

The best food:
_____

Games played:
_____

Something disappointing:
_____

Next time I'll do this differently:
_____

Accomac Historic District
City: Accomac County: Accomack

Plan your trip: https://www.virginia.org/listings/HistoricSites/Accomac/

History:

Things To Do:

- ❑ ADA availability
- ❑ Public Restrooms
- ❑ Gift Shop
- ❑ Museum
- ❑ Visitor Center
- ❑ Picnic areas
- ❑ Chamber of Commerce
- ❑ Monuments
- ❑ Art Galleries
- ❑ Tours
- ❑ Street Art
- ❑ Natural Areas
- ❑ Living History
- ❑ Cemetery
- ❑ Amphitheater

Places I Want to Visit in the Area:

Restaurants:
Boutiques & Shops:
Monuments:
Museums:

Get the Facts

- ❑ Address_____
- _____
- ❑ Phone   757-787-2460
- ❑ Best season to visit
- _____
- ❑ Pet Friendly   Y   N
- ❑ Reservations?   Y   N
- date made_____
- ❑ Distance from home
- miles: _____
- hours: _____

Budget for this trip:

Parking	$
Food	$
Museums	$
Hotel	$
Shopping	$
Total	$

Notes:

Restaurant:

My Experience:

Shopping:

Best Find:

The shop I want to go back to:

Museum:

The coolest thing I learned about this area:

Other:

Notes:

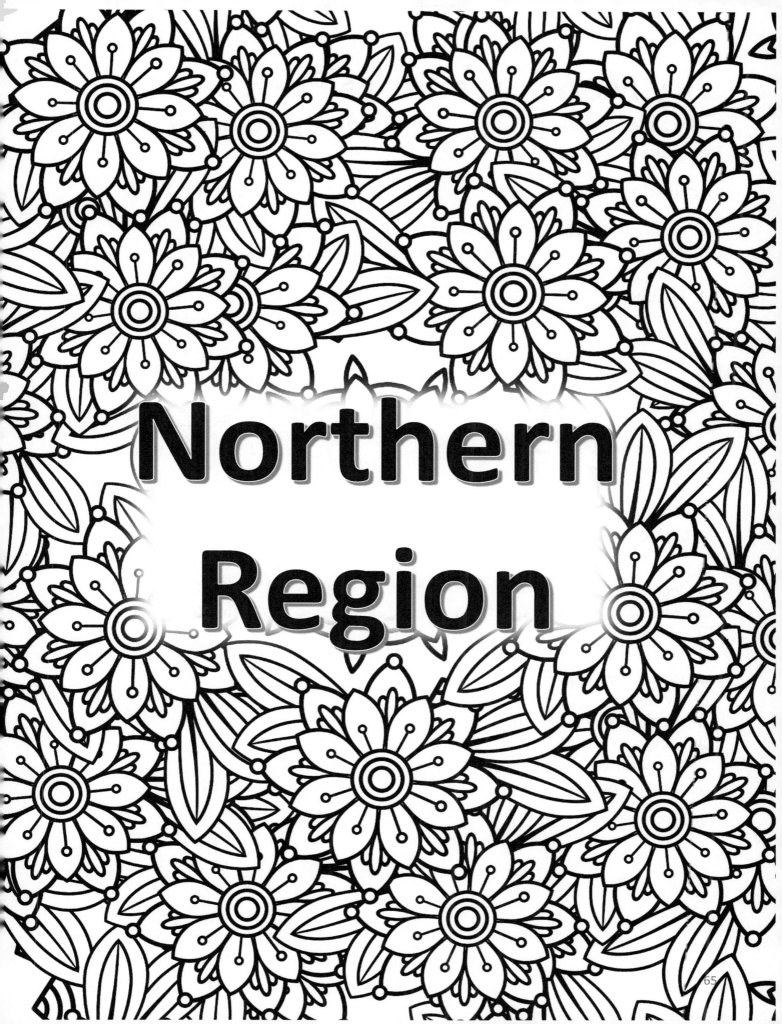
Northern Region

Sky Meadows State Park
City: Delaplane   County: Fauquier

Plan your trip: https://www.dcr.virginia.gov/state-parks/sky-meadows

Activities:

- ☐ Appalachian Trail
- ☐ Archery
- ☐ Biking
- ☐ Boating
- ☐ Camping
- ☐ Fishing
- ☐ Hiking
- ☐ Historic Sites
- ☐ Horseback Riding
- ☐ Hunting
- ☐ Photography
- ☐ Swimming

- ☐ Wildlife & Birding
- ☐
- ☐
- ☐
- ☐
- ☐
- ☐
- ☐
- ☐
- ☐

- ☐
- ☐
- ☐
- ☐
- ☐
- ☐
- ☐
- ☐
- ☐
- ☐
- ☐

Facilities:

- ☐ ADA
- ☐ Picnic sites
- ☐ Restrooms / Showers
- ☐ Trailer Access
- ☐ Visitor center
- ☐ Group Camping
- ☐ RV Camp
- ☐ Rustic Camping
- ☐ Cabins / Yurts / Bunkhouses
- ☐ Day Use Area

Notes:

Get the Facts

- ☐ Phone   540-592-3556
- ☐ Park Hours

  _____

- ☐ Reservations? _____Y _____N

  date made_____

- ☐ Open all year _____Y_____N

  dates_____

- ☐ Check in time _____
- ☐ Check out time _____
- ☐ Pet friendly _____Y _____N
- ☐ Max RV length _____
- ☐ Distance from home

  miles: _____

  hours: _____

- ☐ Address_____

  _____

  _____

Fees:

- ☐ Day Use $ _____
- ☐ Camp Sites $ _____
- ☐ RV Sites $ _____
- ☐ Refund policy

  _____

  _____

  _____

Make It Personal

Trip dates: _____ | The weather was: Sunny Cloudy Rainy Stormy Snowy Foggy Warm Cold

Why I went: _____

_____

How I got there: (circle all that apply) Plane Train Car Bus Bike Hike RV MC

I went with: _____

We stayed in (space, cabin # etc): _____

Most relaxing day: _____

_____

Something funny: _____

_____

Someone we met: _____

_____

Best story told: _____

_____

The kids liked this: _____

_____

The best food: _____

_____

Games played: _____

_____

Something disappointing: _____

_____

Next time I'll do this differently: _____

_____

Leeslvania State Park
City: Woodbridge   County: Prince William

Plan your trip: https://www.dcr.virginia.gov/state-parks/leesylvania

Activities:

- ❑ Appalachian Trail
- ❑ Archery
- ❑ Biking
- ❑ Boating
- ❑ Camping
- ❑ Fishing
- ❑ Hiking
- ❑ Historic Sites
- ❑ Horseback Riding
- ❑ Hunting
- ❑ Photography
- ❑ Swimming

- ❑ Wildlife & Birding
- ❑
- ❑
- ❑
- ❑
- ❑
- ❑
- ❑
- ❑
- ❑

- ❑
- ❑
- ❑
- ❑
- ❑
- ❑
- ❑
- ❑
- ❑
- ❑
- ❑
- ❑

Facilities:

- ❑ ADA
- ❑ Picnic sites
- ❑ Restrooms / Showers
- ❑ Trailer Access
- ❑ Visitor center
- ❑ Group Camping
- ❑ RV Camp
- ❑ Rustic Camping
- ❑ Cabins / Yurts / Bunkhouses
- ❑ Day Use Area

Notes:

Get the Facts

- ❑ Phone   703-730-8205
- ❑ Park Hours

  _____

- ❑ Reservations? ____Y ____N

  date made_____

- ❑ Open all year ____Y____N

  dates_____

- ❑ Check in time _____
- ❑ Check out time _____
- ❑ Pet friendly _____Y _____N
- ❑ Max RV length _____
- ❑ Distance from home

  miles: _____

  hours: _____

- ❑ Address_____

  _____

  _____

Fees:

- ❑ Day Use $ _____
- ❑ Camp Sites $ _____
- ❑ RV Sites $ _____
- ❑ Refund policy

  _____

  _____

  _____

Make It Personal

Trip dates: _____ | The weather was: Sunny Cloudy Rainy Stormy Snowy Foggy Warm Cold

Why I went: _____

_____

How I got there: (circle all that apply)   Plane   Train   Car   Bus   Bike   Hike   RV   MC

I went with: _____

We stayed in (space, cabin # etc): _____

Most relaxing day: _____

_____

Something funny: _____

_____

Someone we met: _____

_____

Best story told: _____

_____

The kids liked this: _____

_____

The best food: _____

_____

Games played: _____

_____

Something disappointing: _____

_____

Next time I'll do this differently: _____

_____

Mason Neck State Park

City: Lorton   County: Fairfax

Plan your trip: https://www.dcr.virginia.gov/state-parks/mason-neck

Activities:

- ❑ Appalachian Trail   ❑
- ❑ Biking   ❑
- ❑ Boating   ❑
- ❑ Fishing   ❑
- ❑ Hiking   ❑
- ❑ Horseback Riding   ❑
- ❑ Wildlife Viewing   ❑
- ❑   ❑
- ❑   ❑
- ❑   ❑
- ❑   ❑

Facilities:

- ❑ ADA   ❑
- ❑ Gift Shop   ❑
- ❑ Museum   ❑
- ❑ Visitor Center   ❑
- ❑ Picnic sites   ❑
- ❑ Restrooms   ❑

Our Visit:

Get the Facts

- ❑ Phone   703-339-2385
- ❑ Park Hours

  _____

- ❑ Reservations? _____Y _____N

  date made_____

- ❑ Open all year? _____Y_____N

  dates_____

- ❑ Dog friendly _____Y _____N

- ❑ Distance from home

  miles: _____

  hours: _____

- ❑ Address_____

  _____

  _____

Fees:

- ❑ Day Use $ _____
- ❑ Refund policy

  _____

  _____

  _____

Notes:

Widewater State Park
City: Stafford   County: Stafford

Plan your trip: https://www.dcr.virginia.gov/state-parks/widewater

Activities:

- ☐ Appalachian Trail   ☐
- ☐ Biking   ☐
- ☐ Boating   ☐
- ☐ Fishing   ☐
- ☐ Hiking   ☐
- ☐ Horseback Riding   ☐
- ☐ Wildlife Viewing   ☐
- ☐   ☐
- ☐   ☐
- ☐   ☐
- ☐   ☐

Facilities:

- ☐ ADA   ☐
- ☐ Gift Shop   ☐
- ☐ Museum   ☐
- ☐ Visitor Center   ☐
- ☐ Picnic sites   ☐
- ☐ Restrooms   ☐

Our Visit:

Get the Facts

- ☐ Phone   540-288-1400
- ☐ Park Hours

  _____

- ☐ Reservations? _____Y _____N

  date made_____

- ☐ Open all year? _____Y_____N

  dates_____

- ☐ Dog friendly _____Y _____N

- ☐ Distance from home

  miles: _____

  hours: _____

- ☐ Address_____

  _____

  _____

Fees:

- ☐ Day Use $ _____
- ☐ Refund policy

  _____

  _____

  _____

Notes:

Fort Myer Historic District
City: Arlington   County: Arlington

Plan your trip: https://militarybases.com/virginia/fort-myer/

History:

Get the Facts

- ❏ Address_____

_____

- ❏ Phone   703-545-6700
- ❏ Best season to visit

_____

- ❏ Pet Friendly   Y   N
- ❏ Reservations?   Y   N

date made_____

- ❏ Distance from home

miles: _____

hours: _____

Things To Do:

- ❏ ADA availability
- ❏ Public Restrooms
- ❏ Gift Shop
- ❏ Museum
- ❏ Visitor Center
- ❏ Picnic areas
- ❏ Chamber of Commerce
- ❏ Monuments
- ❏ Art Galleries
- ❏ Tours
- ❏ Street Art
- ❏ Natural Areas
- ❏ Living History
- ❏ Cemetery
- ❏ Amphitheater

Places I Want to Visit in the Area:

Restaurants:

Boutiques & Shops:

Monuments:

Museums:

Budget for this trip:

Parking	$
Food	$
Museums	$
Hotel	$
Shopping	$
Total	$

Notes:

Restaurant:

My Experience:

Shopping:

Best Find:

The shop I want to go back to:

Museum:

The coolest thing I learned about this area:

Other:

Alexandria Historic District
City: Alexandria   County: Fairfax

Plan your trip: https://www.visitalexandriava.com/old-town-alexandria/

History:

Things To Do:

- ❑ ADA availability
- ❑ Public Restrooms
- ❑ Gift Shop
- ❑ Museum
- ❑ Visitor Center
- ❑ Picnic areas
- ❑ Chamber of Commerce
- ❑ Monuments
- ❑ Art Galleries
- ❑ Tours
- ❑ Street Art
- ❑ Natural Areas
- ❑ Living History
- ❑ Cemetery
- ❑ Amphitheater

Places I Want to Visit in the Area:

Restaurants:

Boutiques & Shops:

Monuments:

Museums:

Get the Facts

- ❑ Address_____
  _____

- ❑ Phone   703-838-5005
- ❑ Best season to visit
  _____

- ❑ Pet Friendly   Y   N
- ❑ Reservations? Y   N

  date made_____

- ❑ Distance from home

  miles: _____

  hours: _____

Budget for this trip:

Parking	$
Food	$
Museums	$
Hotel	$
Shopping	$
Total	$

Notes:

Restaurant:

My Experience:

Shopping:

Best Find:

The shop I want to go back to:

Museum:

The coolest thing I learned about this area:

Other:

Potomac Canal Historic District
City: Great Falls   County: Fairfax

Plan your trip: https://www.nps.gov/places/potomac-canal-historic-district.htm

History:

Get the Facts

- ❑ Address_____

  _____

- ❑ Phone   215-597-5814
- ❑ Best season to visit

  _____

- ❑ Pet Friendly   Y   N
- ❑ Reservations?   Y   N

  date made_____

- ❑ Distance from home

  miles: _____

  hours: _____

Things To Do:

- ❑ ADA availability
- ❑ Public Restrooms
- ❑ Gift Shop
- ❑ Museum
- ❑ Visitor Center
- ❑ Picnic areas
- ❑ Chamber of Commerce
- ❑ Monuments
- ❑ Art Galleries
- ❑ Tours
- ❑ Street Art
- ❑ Natural Areas
- ❑ Living History
- ❑ Cemetery
- ❑ Amphitheater

Places I Want to Visit in the Area:

Restaurants:

Boutiques & Shops:

Monuments:

Museums:

Budget for this trip:

Parking	$
Food	$
Museums	$
Hotel	$
Shopping	$
Total	$

Notes:

Restaurant:

My Experience:

Shopping:

Best Find:

The shop I want to go back to:

Museum:

The coolest thing I learned about this area:

Other:

Historic Herndon

City: Herndon   **County: Fairfax**

Plan your trip: http://herndonhistoricalsociety.org/walkingtourinformation.html

History:

Get the Facts

- ❑ Address_____
  _____
- ❑ Phone   703-435-2520
- ❑ Best season to visit
  _____
- ❑ Pet Friendly   Y   N
- ❑ Reservations?   Y   N
  date made_____
- ❑ Distance from home
  miles: _____
  hours: _____

Things To Do:

- ❑ ADA availability
- ❑ Public Restrooms
- ❑ Gift Shop
- ❑ Museum
- ❑ Visitor Center
- ❑ Picnic areas
- ❑ Chamber of Commerce

- ❑ Monuments
- ❑ Art Galleries
- ❑ Tours
- ❑ Street Art
- ❑ Natural Areas
- ❑ Living History
- ❑ Cemetery
- ❑ Amphitheater

Places I Want to Visit in the Area:

Restaurants:
Boutiques & Shops:
Monuments:
Museums:

Budget for this trip:

Parking	$
Food	$
Museums	$
Hotel	$
Shopping	$
Total	$

Notes:

Restaurant:

My Experience:

Shopping:

Best Find:

The shop I want to go back to:

Museum:

The coolest thing I learned about this area:

Other:

Virginia Piedmont Heritage Area
City: Marshall   County: Fauquier

Plan your trip: https://www.piedmontheritage.org/

History:

Get the Facts

- ❑ Address_____
  _____
- ❑ Phone   540-687-6681
- ❑ Best season to visit
  _____
- ❑ Pet Friendly   Y   N
- ❑ Reservations?   Y   N
  date made_____
- ❑ Distance from home
  miles: _____
  hours: _____

Things To Do:

- ❑ ADA availability
- ❑ Public Restrooms
- ❑ Gift Shop
- ❑ Museum
- ❑ Visitor Center
- ❑ Picnic areas
- ❑ Chamber of Commerce
- ❑ Monuments
- ❑ Art Galleries
- ❑ Tours
- ❑ Street Art
- ❑ Natural Areas
- ❑ Living History
- ❑ Cemetery
- ❑ Amphitheater

Places I Want to Visit in the Area:

Restaurants:
Boutiques & Shops:
Monuments:
Museums:

Budget for this trip:

Parking	$
Food	$
Museums	$
Hotel	$
Shopping	$
Total	$

Notes:

Restaurant:

My Experience:

Shopping:

Best Find:

The shop I want to go back to:

Museum:

The coolest thing I learned about this area:

Other:

Leesburg Historic District
City: Leesburg   County: Loudoun

Plan your trip: http://downtownleesburgva.com/

History:

Get the Facts

- ❏ Address_____

  _____

- ❏ Phone   703-973-6400
- ❏ Best season to visit

  _____

- ❏ Pet Friendly   Y   N
- ❏ Reservations?   Y   N

  date made_____

- ❏ Distance from home

  miles: _____

  hours: _____

Things To Do:

- ❏ ADA availability
- ❏ Public Restrooms
- ❏ Gift Shop
- ❏ Museum
- ❏ Visitor Center
- ❏ Picnic areas
- ❏ Chamber of Commerce
- ❏ Monuments
- ❏ Art Galleries
- ❏ Tours
- ❏ Street Art
- ❏ Natural Areas
- ❏ Living History
- ❏ Cemetery
- ❏ Amphitheater

Places I Want to Visit in the Area:

Restaurants:
Boutiques & Shops:
Monuments:
Museums:

Budget for this trip:

Parking	$
Food	$
Museums	$
Hotel	$
Shopping	$
Total	$

Notes:

Restaurant:

My Experience:

Shopping:

Best Find:

The shop I want to go back to:

Museum:

The coolest thing I learned about this area:

Other:

Waterford Historic District
City: Waterford   County: Loudoun

Plan your trip: https://www.nps.gov/places/waterford-historic-district.htm

History:

Things To Do:

- ❏ ADA availability
- ❏ Public Restrooms
- ❏ Gift Shop
- ❏ Museum
- ❏ Visitor Center
- ❏ Picnic areas
- ❏ Chamber of Commerce
- ❏ Monuments
- ❏ Art Galleries
- ❏ Tours
- ❏ Street Art
- ❏ Natural Areas
- ❏ Living History
- ❏ Cemetery
- ❏ Amphitheater

Places I Want to Visit in the Area:

Restaurants:

Boutiques & Shops:

Monuments:

Museums:

Get the Facts

- ❏ Address_____
  _____
- ❏ Phone   215-597-5814
- ❏ Best season to visit
  _____
- ❏ Pet Friendly   Y   N
- ❏ Reservations?   Y   N
  date made_____
- ❏ Distance from home
  miles: _____
  hours: _____

Budget for this trip:

Parking	$
Food	$
Museums	$
Hotel	$
Shopping	$
Total	$

Notes:

Restaurant:

My Experience:

Shopping:

Best Find:

The shop I want to go back to:

Museum:

The coolest thing I learned about this area:

Other:

Notes:

Douthat State Park
City: Millboro   County: Bath

Plan your trip: https://www.dcr.virginia.gov/state-parks/douthat

Activities:

- ❏ Appalachian Trail
- ❏ Archery
- ❏ Biking
- ❏ Boating
- ❏ Camping
- ❏ Fishing
- ❏ Hiking
- ❏ Historic Sites
- ❏ Horseback Riding
- ❏ Hunting
- ❏ Photography
- ❏ Swimming
- ❏ Wildlife & Birding

Facilities:

- ❏ ADA
- ❏ Picnic sites
- ❏ Restrooms / Showers
- ❏ Trailer Access
- ❏ Visitor center
- ❏ Group Camping
- ❏ RV Camp
- ❏ Rustic Camping
- ❏ Cabins / Yurts / Bunkhouses
- ❏ Day Use Area

Notes:

Get the Facts

- ❏ Phone   540-862-8100
- ❏ Park Hours _____
- ❏ Reservations? ____Y ____N

  date made_____
- ❏ Open all year ____Y____N

  dates_____
- ❏ Check in time _____
- ❏ Check out time _____
- ❏ Pet friendly _____Y _____N
- ❏ Max RV length _____
- ❏ Distance from home

  miles: _____

  hours: _____
- ❏ Address_____

  _____

  _____

Fees:

- ❏ Day Use $ _____
- ❏ Camp Sites $ _____
- ❏ RV Sites $ _____
- ❏ Refund policy

  _____

  _____

  _____

Make It Personal

Trip dates: _____ | The weather was: Sunny Cloudy Rainy Stormy Snowy Foggy Warm Cold

Why I went: _____

_____

How I got there: (circle all that apply)   Plane   Train   Car   Bus   Bike   Hike   RV   MC

I went with: _____

We stayed in (space, cabin # etc): _____

Most relaxing day: _____

_____

Something funny: _____

_____

Someone we met: _____

_____

Best story told: _____

_____

The kids liked this: _____

_____

The best food: _____

_____

Games played: _____

_____

Something disappointing: _____

_____

Next time I'll do this differently: _____

_____

Barbours Creek Wilderness
City: Potts Mountain   County: Craig

Plan your trip: http://www.vawilderness.org/barbours-creek-wilderness.html

Activities:

- ❑ Appalachian Trail
- ❑ Archery
- ❑ Biking
- ❑ Boating
- ❑ Camping
- ❑ Fishing
- ❑ Hiking
- ❑ Historic Sites
- ❑ Horseback Riding
- ❑ Hunting
- ❑ Photography
- ❑ Swimming

- ❑ Wildlife & Birding
- ❑
- ❑
- ❑
- ❑
- ❑
- ❑
- ❑
- ❑
- ❑
- ❑

- ❑
- ❑
- ❑
- ❑
- ❑
- ❑
- ❑
- ❑
- ❑
- ❑
- ❑
- ❑

Facilities:

- ❑ ADA
- ❑ Picnic sites
- ❑ Restrooms / Showers
- ❑ Trailer Access
- ❑ Visitor center
- ❑ Group Camping
- ❑ RV Camp
- ❑ Rustic Camping
- ❑ Cabins / Yurts / Bunkhouses
- ❑ Day Use Area

Notes:

Get the Facts

- ❑ Phone   540-464-1661
- ❑ Park Hours

  _____

- ❑ Reservations? ____Y ____N

  date made_____

- ❑ Open all year ____Y_____N

  dates_____

- ❑ Check in time _____
- ❑ Check out time _____
- ❑ Pet friendly _____Y _____N
- ❑ Max RV length _____
- ❑ Distance from home

  miles: _____

  hours: _____

- ❑ Address_____

  _____

  _____

Fees:

- ❑ Day Use $ _____
- ❑ Camp Sites $ _____
- ❑ RV Sites $ _____
- ❑ Refund policy

  _____

  _____

  _____

Make It Personal

Trip dates: _____ | The weather was: Sunny Cloudy Rainy Stormy Snowy Foggy Warm Cold

Why I went:
_____

How I got there: (circle all that apply)   Plane   Train   Car   Bus   Bike   Hike   RV   MC

I went with:
_____

We stayed in (space, cabin # etc):
_____

Most relaxing day:
_____

Something funny:
_____

Someone we met:
_____

Best story told:
_____

The kids liked this:
_____

The best food:
_____

Games played:
_____

Something disappointing:
_____

Next time I'll do this differently:
_____

Shawvers Run Wilderness
City: Potts Mountain   County: Craig
Plan your trip: http://www.vawilderness.org/shawvers-run-wilderness.html

Activities:

- ❑ Appalachian Trail
- ❑ Archery
- ❑ Biking
- ❑ Boating
- ❑ Camping
- ❑ Fishing
- ❑ Hiking
- ❑ Historic Sites
- ❑ Horseback Riding
- ❑ Hunting
- ❑ Photography
- ❑ Swimming

- ❑ Wildlife & Birding
- ❑
- ❑
- ❑
- ❑
- ❑
- ❑
- ❑
- ❑
- ❑
- ❑

- ❑
- ❑
- ❑
- ❑
- ❑
- ❑
- ❑
- ❑
- ❑
- ❑
- ❑

Facilities:

- ❑ ADA
- ❑ Picnic sites
- ❑ Restrooms / Showers
- ❑ Trailer Access
- ❑ Visitor center
- ❑ Group Camping
- ❑ RV Camp
- ❑ Rustic Camping
- ❑ Cabins / Yurts / Bunkhouses
- ❑ Day Use Area

Notes:

Get the Facts

- ❑ Phone   540-464-1661
- ❑ Park Hours

  _____

- ❑ Reservations? ____Y ____N

  date made_____

- ❑ Open all year ____Y____N

  dates_____

- ❑ Check in time _____
- ❑ Check out time _____
- ❑ Pet friendly _____Y _____N
- ❑ Max RV length _____
- ❑ Distance from home

  miles: _____

  hours: _____

- ❑ Address_____

  _____

  _____

Fees:

- ❑ Day Use $ _____
- ❑ Camp Sites $ _____
- ❑ RV Sites $ _____
- ❑ Refund policy

  _____

  _____

  _____

Make It Personal

Trip dates: _____ | The weather was: Sunny Cloudy Rainy Stormy Snowy Foggy Warm Cold

Why I went: _____

How I got there: (circle all that apply) Plane Train Car Bus Bike Hike RV MC

I went with: _____

We stayed in (space, cabin # etc): _____

Most relaxing day: _____

Something funny: _____

Someone we met: _____

Best story told: _____

The kids liked this: _____

The best food: _____

Games played: _____

Something disappointing: _____

Next time I'll do this differently: _____

Cave Mountain Lake Recreation Area
City: Natural Bridge Station   County: Rockbridge

Plan your trip: https://www.fs.usda.gov/recarea/gwj/recreation/beaches-dunes/recarea/?recid=73641&actid=20

Activities:

- ☐ Appalachian Trail
- ☐ Archery
- ☐ Biking
- ☐ Boating
- ☐ Camping
- ☐ Fishing
- ☐ Hiking
- ☐ Historic Sites
- ☐ Horseback Riding
- ☐ Hunting
- ☐ Photography
- ☐ Swimming

- ☐ Wildlife & Birding
- ☐
- ☐
- ☐
- ☐
- ☐
- ☐
- ☐
- ☐
- ☐

- ☐
- ☐
- ☐
- ☐
- ☐
- ☐
- ☐
- ☐
- ☐
- ☐
- ☐

Facilities:

- ☐ ADA
- ☐ Picnic sites
- ☐ Restrooms / Showers
- ☐ Trailer Access
- ☐ Visitor center
- ☐ Group Camping
- ☐ RV Camp
- ☐ Rustic Camping
- ☐ Cabins / Yurts / Bunkhouses
- ☐ Day Use Area

Notes:

Get the Facts

- ☐ Phone   540-291-2188
- ☐ Park Hours

  _____

- ☐ Reservations? _____Y _____N

  date made_____

- ☐ Open all year _____Y_____N

  dates_____

- ☐ Check in time _____
- ☐ Check out time _____
- ☐ Pet friendly _____Y _____N
- ☐ Max RV length _____
- ☐ Distance from home

  miles: _____

  hours: _____

- ☐ Address_____

  _____

  _____

Fees:

- ☐ Day Use $ _____
- ☐ Camp Sites $ _____
- ☐ RV Sites $ _____
- ☐ Refund policy

  _____

  _____

  _____

Make It Personal

Trip dates: _____

The weather was: Sunny Cloudy Rainy Stormy Snowy Foggy Warm Cold

Why I went: _____

_____

How I got there: (circle all that apply) Plane Train Car Bus Bike Hike RV MC

I went with: _____

We stayed in (space, cabin # etc): _____

Most relaxing day: _____

_____

Something funny: _____

_____

Someone we met: _____

_____

Best story told: _____

_____

The kids liked this: _____

_____

The best food: _____

_____

Games played: _____

_____

Something disappointing: _____

_____

Next time I'll do this differently: _____

_____

Ramsey's Draft Wilderness

City: West Augusta   County: Augusta

Plan your trip: http://www.vawilderness.org/ramseys-draft-hike.html

Activities:

- ❑ Appalachian Trail   ❑
- ❑ Biking   ❑
- ❑ Boating   ❑
- ❑ Fishing   ❑
- ❑ Hiking   ❑
- ❑ Horseback Riding   ❑
- ❑ Wildlife Viewing   ❑
- ❑   ❑
- ❑   ❑
- ❑   ❑
- ❑   ❑

Facilities:

- ❑ ADA   ❑
- ❑ Gift Shop   ❑
- ❑ Museum   ❑
- ❑ Visitor Center   ❑
- ❑ Picnic sites   ❑
- ❑ Restrooms   ❑

Our Visit:

Get the Facts

- ❑ Phone   540-265-5100
- ❑ Park Hours

   _____

- ❑ Reservations? _____Y _____N

   date made_____

- ❑ Open all year? _____Y_____N

   dates_____

- ❑ Dog friendly _____Y _____N

- ❑ Distance from home

   miles: _____

   hours: _____

- ❑ Address_____

   _____

   _____

Fees:

- ❑ Day Use $ _____
- ❑ Refund policy

   _____

   _____

   _____

Notes:

Rough Mountain Wilderness
City: Millboro   County: Bath

Plan your trip: http://www.vawilderness.org/rough-mountain.html

Activities:

- ☐ Appalachian Trail
- ☐ Biking
- ☐ Boating
- ☐ Fishing
- ☐ Hiking
- ☐ Horseback Riding
- ☐ Wildlife Viewing
- ☐
- ☐
- ☐
- ☐

☐ ☐ ☐ ☐ ☐ ☐ ☐ ☐ ☐ ☐ ☐

Facilities:

- ☐ ADA
- ☐ Gift Shop
- ☐ Museum
- ☐ Visitor Center
- ☐ Picnic sites
- ☐ Restrooms

☐ ☐ ☐ ☐ ☐ ☐

Our Visit:

Get the Facts

- ☐ Phone   540-464-1661
- ☐ Park Hours

  _____

- ☐ Reservations? _____Y _____N

  date made_____

- ☐ Open all year? _____Y_____N

  dates_____

- ☐ Dog friendly _____Y _____N

- ☐ Distance from home

  miles: _____

  hours: _____

- ☐ Address_____

  _____

  _____

Fees:

- ☐ Day Use $ _____
- ☐ Refund policy

  _____

  _____

  _____

Notes:

Rich Hole Wilderness

City: Goshen **County: Rockbridge**

Plan your trip: http://www.vawilderness.org/rich-hole-wilderness.html

Activities:

- ❑ Appalachian Trail ❑
- ❑ Biking ❑
- ❑ Boating ❑
- ❑ Fishing ❑
- ❑ Hiking ❑
- ❑ Horseback Riding ❑
- ❑ Wildlife Viewing ❑
- ❑ ❑
- ❑ ❑
- ❑ ❑
- ❑ ❑

Facilities:

- ❑ ADA ❑
- ❑ Gift Shop ❑
- ❑ Museum ❑
- ❑ Visitor Center ❑
- ❑ Picnic sites ❑
- ❑ Restrooms ❑

Our Visit:

Get the Facts

- ❑ Phone   540-464-1661
- ❑ Park Hours

  _____

- ❑ Reservations? ____Y ____N

  date made_____

- ❑ Open all year? ____Y____N

  dates_____

- ❑ Dog friendly _____Y _____N

- ❑ Distance from home

  miles: _____

  hours: _____

- ❑ Address_____

  _____

  _____

Fees:

- ❑ Day Use $ _____
- ❑ Refund policy

  _____

  _____

  _____

Notes:

Thunder Ridge Wilderness
City: Natural Bridge Station   County: Rockbridge

Plan your trip: http://www.vawilderness.org/thunder-ridge-wilderness.html

Activities:

- ❑ Appalachian Trail   ❑
- ❑ Biking   ❑
- ❑ Boating   ❑
- ❑ Fishing   ❑
- ❑ Hiking   ❑
- ❑ Horseback Riding   ❑
- ❑ Wildlife Viewing   ❑
- ❑   ❑
- ❑   ❑
- ❑   ❑
- ❑   ❑

Facilities:

- ❑ ADA   ❑
- ❑ Gift Shop   ❑
- ❑ Museum   ❑
- ❑ Visitor Center   ❑
- ❑ Picnic sites   ❑
- ❑ Restrooms   ❑

Our Visit:

Get the Facts

- ❑ Phone   540-464-1661
- ❑ Park Hours

_____

- ❑ Reservations? _____Y _____N

date made_____

- ❑ Open all year? _____Y_____N

dates_____

- ❑ Dog friendly _____Y _____N

- ❑ Distance from home

miles: _____

hours: _____

- ❑ Address_____

_____

_____

Fees:

- ❑ Day Use $ _____
- ❑ Refund policy

_____

_____

_____

Notes:

St. Mary's Wilderness
City: Raphine   County: Rockbridge
Plan your trip: www.vawilderness.org/st-marys-wilderness.html

Activities:

- ❑ Appalachian Trail   ❑
- ❑ Biking   ❑
- ❑ Boating   ❑
- ❑ Fishing   ❑
- ❑ Hiking   ❑
- ❑ Horseback Riding   ❑
- ❑ Wildlife Viewing   ❑
- ❑   ❑
- ❑   ❑
- ❑   ❑
- ❑   ❑

Facilities:

- ❑ ADA   ❑
- ❑ Gift Shop   ❑
- ❑ Museum   ❑
- ❑ Visitor Center   ❑
- ❑ Picnic sites   ❑
- ❑ Restrooms   ❑

Our Visit:

Get the Facts

- ❑ Phone   540-291-2188
- ❑ Park Hours

  _____

- ❑ Reservations? ____Y ____N

  date made_____

- ❑ Open all year? ____Y____N

  dates_____

- ❑ Dog friendly _____Y _____N

- ❑ Distance from home

  miles: _____

  hours: _____

- ❑ Address_____

  _____

  _____

Fees:

- ❑ Day Use $ _____
- ❑ Refund policy

  _____

  _____

  _____

Notes:

Natural Bridge State Park
City: Natural Bridge   County: Rockbridge

Plan your trip: https://www.dcr.virginia.gov/state-parks/natural-bridge

Activities:

- ❑ Appalachian Trail   ❑
- ❑ Biking   ❑
- ❑ Boating   ❑
- ❑ Fishing   ❑
- ❑ Hiking   ❑
- ❑ Horseback Riding   ❑
- ❑ Wildlife Viewing   ❑
- ❑   ❑
- ❑   ❑
- ❑   ❑
- ❑   ❑

Facilities:

- ❑ ADA   ❑
- ❑ Gift Shop   ❑
- ❑ Museum   ❑
- ❑ Visitor Center   ❑
- ❑ Picnic sites   ❑
- ❑ Restrooms   ❑

Our Visit:

Get the Facts

- ❑ Phone   540-291-1326
- ❑ Park Hours

  _____

- ❑ Reservations? _____Y _____N

  date made_____

- ❑ Open all year? _____Y_____N

  dates_____

- ❑ Dog friendly _____Y _____N

- ❑ Distance from home

  miles: _____

  hours: _____

- ❑ Address_____

  _____

  _____

Fees:

- ❑ Day Use $ _____
- ❑ Refund policy

  _____

  _____

  _____

Notes:

James River Face Wilderness
City: Natural Bridge Station   County: Rockbridge
Plan your trip: http://www.vawilderness.org/james-river-face-wilderness.html

Activities:

- ❏ Appalachian Trail
- ❏ Biking
- ❏ Boating
- ❏ Fishing
- ❏ Hiking
- ❏ Horseback Riding
- ❏ Wildlife Viewing
- ❏
- ❏
- ❏
- ❏

❏ ❏ ❏ ❏ ❏ ❏ ❏ ❏ ❏ ❏ ❏

Facilities:

- ❏ ADA
- ❏ Gift Shop
- ❏ Museum
- ❏ Visitor Center
- ❏ Picnic sites
- ❏ Restrooms

❏ ❏ ❏ ❏ ❏ ❏

Our Visit:

Get the Facts

- ❏ Phone   540-464-1661
- ❏ Park Hours

  _____

- ❏ Reservations? _____Y _____N

  date made_____

- ❏ Open all year? _____Y_____N

  dates_____

- ❏ Dog friendly _____Y _____N

- ❏ Distance from home

  miles: _____

  hours: _____

- ❏ Address_____

  _____

  _____

Fees:

- ❏ Day Use $ _____
- ❏ Refund policy

  _____

  _____

  _____

Notes:

Seven Bends State Park
City: Woodstock   County: Shenandoah

Plan your trip: https://www.dcr.virginia.gov/state-parks/seven-bends

Activities:

- ❑ Appalachian Trail   ❑
- ❑ Biking   ❑
- ❑ Boating   ❑
- ❑ Fishing   ❑
- ❑ Hiking   ❑
- ❑ Horseback Riding   ❑
- ❑ Wildlife Viewing   ❑
- ❑   ❑
- ❑   ❑
- ❑   ❑
- ❑   ❑

Facilities:

- ❑ ADA   ❑
- ❑ Gift Shop   ❑
- ❑ Museum   ❑
- ❑ Visitor Center ❑
- ❑ Picnic sites   ❑
- ❑ Restrooms   ❑

Our Visit:

Get the Facts

- ❑ Phone   540-622-6840
- ❑ Park Hours

  _____

- ❑ Reservations? ____Y ____N

  date made_____

- ❑ Open all year? ____Y____N

  dates_____

- ❑ Dog friendly _____Y _____N

- ❑ Distance from home

  miles: _____

  hours: _____

- ❑ Address_____

  _____

  _____

Fees:

- ❑ Day Use $ _____
- ❑ Refund policy

  _____

  _____

  _____

Notes:

Historic Downtown Staunton

City: Staunton   County: Augusta

Plan your trip: https://www.stauntondowntown.org/

History:

Things To Do:

- ❑ ADA availability
- ❑ Public Restrooms
- ❑ Gift Shop
- ❑ Museum
- ❑ Visitor Center
- ❑ Picnic areas
- ❑ Chamber of Commerce
- ❑ Monuments
- ❑ Art Galleries
- ❑ Tours
- ❑ Street Art
- ❑ Natural Areas
- ❑ Living History
- ❑ Cemetery
- ❑ Amphitheater

Places I Want to Visit in the Area:

Restaurants:

Boutiques & Shops:

Monuments:

Museums:

Get the Facts

- ❑ Address_____

  _____

- ❑ Phone   540-332-3867
- ❑ Best season to visit

  _____

- ❑ Pet Friendly   Y   N
- ❑ Reservations?   Y   N

  date made_____

- ❑ Distance from home

  miles: _____

  hours: _____

Budget for this trip:

Parking	$
Food	$
Museums	$
Hotel	$
Shopping	$
Total	$

Notes:

Restaurant:

My Experience:

Shopping:

Best Find:

The shop I want to go back to:

Museum:

The coolest thing I learned about this area:

Other:

Historic Buchanan

City: Buchanan   County: Botetourt

Plan your trip: https://www.townofbuchanan.com/

History:

Get the Facts

- ❑ Address_____
  _____

- ❑ Phone   540-254-1212
- ❑ Best season to visit
  _____

- ❑ Pet Friendly   Y   N
- ❑ Reservations?   Y   N
  date made_____

- ❑ Distance from home
  miles: _____
  hours: _____

Things To Do:

- ❑ ADA availability
- ❑ Public Restrooms
- ❑ Gift Shop
- ❑ Museum
- ❑ Visitor Center
- ❑ Picnic areas
- ❑ Chamber of Commerce

- ❑ Monuments
- ❑ Art Galleries
- ❑ Tours
- ❑ Street Art
- ❑ Natural Areas
- ❑ Living History
- ❑ Cemetery
- ❑ Amphitheater

Places I Want to Visit in the Area:

Restaurants:

Boutiques & Shops:

Monuments:

Museums:

Budget for this trip:

Parking	$
Food	$
Museums	$
Hotel	$
Shopping	$
Total	$

Notes:

Restaurant:

My Experience:

Shopping:

Best Find:

The shop I want to go back to:

Museum:

The coolest thing I learned about this area:

Other:

Skyline Drive Historic District
City: Luray   County: Page

Plan your trip: https://www.nps.gov/shen/learn/historyculture/skylinedrive.htm

History:

Things To Do:

- ❑ ADA availability
- ❑ Public Restrooms
- ❑ Gift Shop
- ❑ Museum
- ❑ Visitor Center
- ❑ Picnic areas
- ❑ Chamber of Commerce

- ❑ Monuments
- ❑ Art Galleries
- ❑ Tours
- ❑ Street Art
- ❑ Natural Areas
- ❑ Living History
- ❑ Cemetery
- ❑ Amphitheater

Places I Want to Visit in the Area:

Restaurants:
Boutiques & Shops:
Monuments:
Museums:

Get the Facts

- ❑ Address_____

  _____

- ❑ Phone   540-999-3500
- ❑ Best season to visit

  _____

- ❑ Pet Friendly   Y   N
- ❑ Reservations?   Y   N

  date made_____

- ❑ Distance from home

  miles: _____

  hours: _____

Budget for this trip:

Parking	$
Food	$
Museums	$
Hotel	$
Shopping	$
Total	$

Notes:

Restaurant:

My Experience:

Shopping:

Best Find:

The shop I want to go back to:

Museum:

The coolest thing I learned about this area:

Other:

Virginia Military Institute HD
City: Lexington   County: Rockbridge

Plan your trip: https://www.vmi.edu/about/history/

History:

Get the Facts

- ❑ Address_____
- _____
- ❑ Phone   540-464-7230
- ❑ Best season to visit
- _____
- ❑ Pet Friendly   Y   N
- ❑ Reservations?   Y   N
- date made_____
- ❑ Distance from home
- miles: _____
- hours: _____

Things To Do:

- ❑ ADA availability
- ❑ Public Restrooms
- ❑ Gift Shop
- ❑ Museum
- ❑ Visitor Center
- ❑ Picnic areas
- ❑ Chamber of Commerce

- ❑ Monuments
- ❑ Art Galleries
- ❑ Tours
- ❑ Street Art
- ❑ Natural Areas
- ❑ Living History
- ❑ Cemetery
- ❑ Amphitheater

Places I Want to Visit in the Area:

Restaurants:

Boutiques & Shops:

Monuments:

Museums:

Budget for this trip:

Parking	$
Food	$
Museums	$
Hotel	$
Shopping	$
Total	$

Notes:

Restaurant:

My Experience:

Shopping:

Best Find:

The shop I want to go back to:

Museum:

The coolest thing I learned about this area:

Other:

Historic New Market

City: New Market   County: Shenandoah

Plan your trip: https://www.newmarketvirginia.com/visitors/area-attractions/

History:

Things To Do:

- ADA availability
- Public Restrooms
- Gift Shop
- Museum
- Visitor Center
- Picnic areas
- Chamber of Commerce
- Monuments
- Art Galleries
- Tours
- Street Art
- Natural Areas
- Living History
- Cemetery
- Amphitheater

Places I Want to Visit in the Area:

Restaurants:
Boutiques & Shops:
Monuments:
Museums:

Get the Facts

- Address_____

  _____

- Phone   540-740-3432
- Best season to visit

  _____

- Pet Friendly   Y   N
- Reservations?   Y   N

  date made_____

- Distance from home

  miles: _____

  hours: _____

Budget for this trip:

Parking	$
Food	$
Museums	$
Hotel	$
Shopping	$
Total	$

Notes:

Restaurant:

My Experience:

Shopping:

Best Find:

The shop I want to go back to:

Museum:

The coolest thing I learned about this area:

Other:

Shenandoah Valley Battlefields NHD
City: New Market   County: Shenandoah

Plan your trip: https://www.shenandoahatwar.org/visit/

History:

Things To Do:

- ☐ ADA availability
- ☐ Public Restrooms
- ☐ Gift Shop
- ☐ Museum
- ☐ Visitor Center
- ☐ Picnic areas
- ☐ Chamber of Commerce
- ☐ Monuments
- ☐ Art Galleries
- ☐ Tours
- ☐ Street Art
- ☐ Natural Areas
- ☐ Living History
- ☐ Cemetery
- ☐ Amphitheater

Places I Want to Visit in the Area:

Restaurants:

Boutiques & Shops:

Monuments:

Museums:

Get the Facts

- ☐ Address_____
  _____
- ☐ Phone   540-740-4545
- ☐ Best season to visit
  _____
- ☐ Pet Friendly   Y   N
- ☐ Reservations?   Y   N
  date made_____
- ☐ Distance from home
  miles: _____
  hours: _____

Budget for this trip:

Parking	$
Food	$
Museums	$
Hotel	$
Shopping	$
Total	$

Notes:

Restaurant:

My Experience:

Shopping:

Best Find:

The shop I want to go back to:

Museum:

The coolest thing I learned about this area:

Other:

Thunderbird Archaeological District
City: Limeton   County: Warren

Plan your trip: https://accessgenealogy.com/virginia/the-archaeological-evidence-in-shenandoah-valley.htm

History:

Things To Do:

- ☐ ADA availability
- ☐ Public Restrooms
- ☐ Gift Shop
- ☐ Museum
- ☐ Visitor Center
- ☐ Picnic areas
- ☐ Chamber of Commerce
- ☐ Monuments
- ☐ Art Galleries
- ☐ Tours
- ☐ Street Art
- ☐ Natural Areas
- ☐ Living History
- ☐ Cemetery
- ☐ Amphitheater

Places I Want to Visit in the Area:

Restaurants:

Boutiques & Shops:

Monuments:

Museums:

Get the Facts

- ☐ Address_____
  _____
- ☐ Phone
- ☐ Best season to visit
  _____
- ☐ Pet Friendly   Y   N
- ☐ Reservations?   Y   N
  date made_____
- ☐ Distance from home
  miles: _____
  hours: _____

Budget for this trip:

Parking	$
Food	$
Museums	$
Hotel	$
Shopping	$
Total	$

Notes:

Restaurant:

My Experience:

Shopping:

Best Find:

The shop I want to go back to:

Museum:

The coolest thing I learned about this area:

Other:

Notes:

Breaks Interstate State Park

City: Breaks   County: Dickenson

Plan your trip: http://www.breakspark.com/

Activities:

- ❑ Appalachian Trail
- ❑ Archery
- ❑ Biking
- ❑ Boating
- ❑ Camping
- ❑ Fishing
- ❑ Hiking
- ❑ Historic Sites
- ❑ Horseback Riding
- ❑ Hunting
- ❑ Photography
- ❑ Swimming

- ❑ Wildlife & Birding
- ❑
- ❑
- ❑
- ❑
- ❑
- ❑
- ❑
- ❑
- ❑

- ❑
- ❑
- ❑
- ❑
- ❑
- ❑
- ❑
- ❑
- ❑
- ❑
- ❑

Facilities:

- ❑ ADA
- ❑ Picnic sites
- ❑ Restrooms / Showers
- ❑ Trailer Access
- ❑ Visitor center
- ❑ Group Camping
- ❑ RV Camp
- ❑ Rustic Camping
- ❑ Cabins / Yurts / Bunkhouses
- ❑ Day Use Area

Notes:

Get the Facts

- ❑ Phone   276-865-4413
- ❑ Park Hours
  _____
- ❑ Reservations? _____ Y _____ N
  date made_____
- ❑ Open all year _____ Y _____ N
  dates_____
- ❑ Check in time _____
- ❑ Check out time _____
- ❑ Pet friendly _____ Y _____ N
- ❑ Max RV length _____
- ❑ Distance from home
  miles: _____
  hours: _____
- ❑ Address_____
  _____
  _____

Fees:

- ❑ Day Use $ _____
- ❑ Camp Sites $ _____
- ❑ RV Sites $ _____
- ❑ Refund policy
  _____
  _____
  _____

Make It Personal

Trip dates: _____ | The weather was: Sunny Cloudy Rainy Stormy Snowy Foggy Warm Cold

Why I went: _____

How I got there: (circle all that apply) Plane Train Car Bus Bike Hike RV MC

I went with: _____

We stayed in (space, cabin # etc): _____

Most relaxing day: _____

Something funny: _____

Someone we met: _____

Best story told: _____

The kids liked this: _____

The best food: _____

Games played: _____

Something disappointing: _____

Next time I'll do this differently: _____

Grayson Highlands State Park
City: Mouth of Wilson   County: Grayson

Plan your trip: https://www.dcr.virginia.gov/state-parks/grayson-highlands

Activities:

- ❑ Appalachian Trail
- ❑ Archery
- ❑ Biking
- ❑ Boating
- ❑ Camping
- ❑ Fishing
- ❑ Hiking
- ❑ Historic Sites
- ❑ Horseback Riding
- ❑ Hunting
- ❑ Photography
- ❑ Swimming
- ❑ Wildlife & Birding
- ❑
- ❑
- ❑
- ❑
- ❑
- ❑
- ❑
- ❑
- ❑

Facilities:

- ❑ ADA
- ❑ Picnic sites
- ❑ Restrooms / Showers
- ❑ Trailer Access
- ❑ Visitor center
- ❑ Group Camping
- ❑ RV Camp
- ❑ Rustic Camping
- ❑ Cabins / Yurts / Bunkhouses
- ❑ Day Use Area

Notes:

Get the Facts

- ❑ Phone   276-579-7092
- ❑ Park Hours

  _____

- ❑ Reservations? _____Y _____N

  date made_____

- ❑ Open all year _____Y_____N

  dates_____

- ❑ Check in time _____
- ❑ Check out time _____
- ❑ Pet friendly _____Y _____N
- ❑ Max RV length _____
- ❑ Distance from home

  miles: _____

  hours: _____

- ❑ Address_____

  _____

  _____

Fees:

- ❑ Day Use $ _____
- ❑ Camp Sites $ _____
- ❑ RV Sites $ _____
- ❑ Refund policy

  _____

  _____

  _____

Make It Personal

Trip dates: | The weather was: Sunny Cloudy Rainy Stormy Snowy Foggy Warm Cold

Why I went:

How I got there: (circle all that apply)   Plane   Train   Car   Bus   Bike   Hike   RV   MC

I went with:

We stayed in (space, cabin # etc):

Most relaxing day:

Something funny:

Someone we met:

Best story told:

The kids liked this:

The best food:

Games played:

Something disappointing:

Next time I'll do this differently:

Lewis Fork Wilderness
City: Troutdale   County: Grayson

Plan your trip: http://www.vawilderness.org/lewis-fork-wilderness.html

Activities:

- ❏ Appalachian Trail
- ❏ Archery
- ❏ Biking
- ❏ Boating
- ❏ Camping
- ❏ Fishing
- ❏ Hiking
- ❏ Historic Sites
- ❏ Horseback Riding
- ❏ Hunting
- ❏ Photography
- ❏ Swimming

- ❏ Wildlife & Birding
- ❏
- ❏
- ❏
- ❏
- ❏
- ❏
- ❏
- ❏
- ❏

- ❏
- ❏
- ❏
- ❏
- ❏
- ❏
- ❏
- ❏
- ❏
- ❏
- ❏
- ❏

Facilities:

- ❏ ADA
- ❏ Picnic sites
- ❏ Restrooms / Showers
- ❏ Trailer Access
- ❏ Visitor center
- ❏ Group Camping
- ❏ RV Camp
- ❏ Rustic Camping
- ❏ Cabins / Yurts / Bunkhouses
- ❏ Day Use Area

Notes:

Get the Facts

- ❏ Phone   540-464-1661
- ❏ Park Hours

  _____

- ❏ Reservations? _____Y _____N

  date made_____

- ❏ Open all year _____Y_____N

  dates_____

- ❏ Check in time _____
- ❏ Check out time _____
- ❏ Pet friendly _____Y _____N
- ❏ Max RV length _____
- ❏ Distance from home

  miles: _____

  hours: _____

- ❏ Address_____

  _____

  _____

Fees:

- ❏ Day Use $ _____
- ❏ Camp Sites $ _____
- ❏ RV Sites $ _____
- ❏ Refund policy

  _____

  _____

  _____

Make It Personal

Trip dates: | The weather was: Sunny Cloudy Rainy Stormy Snowy Foggy Warm Cold

Why I went:

How I got there: (circle all that apply)   Plane   Train   Car   Bus   Bike   Hike   RV   MC

I went with:

We stayed in (space, cabin # etc):

Most relaxing day:

Something funny:

Someone we met:

Best story told:

The kids liked this:

The best food:

Games played:

Something disappointing:

Next time I'll do this differently:

Wilderness Road State Park
City: Ewing   County: Lee
Plan your trip: https://www.dcr.virginia.gov/state-parks/wilderness-road

Activities:

- ❑ Appalachian Trail
- ❑ Archery
- ❑ Biking
- ❑ Boating
- ❑ Camping
- ❑ Fishing
- ❑ Hiking
- ❑ Historic Sites
- ❑ Horseback Riding
- ❑ Hunting
- ❑ Photography
- ❑ Swimming

- ❑ Wildlife & Birding
- ❑
- ❑
- ❑
- ❑
- ❑
- ❑
- ❑
- ❑

- ❑
- ❑
- ❑
- ❑
- ❑
- ❑
- ❑
- ❑
- ❑
- ❑
- ❑
- ❑

Facilities:

- ❑ ADA
- ❑ Picnic sites
- ❑ Restrooms / Showers
- ❑ Trailer Access
- ❑ Visitor center
- ❑ Group Camping
- ❑ RV Camp
- ❑ Rustic Camping
- ❑ Cabins / Yurts / Bunkhouses
- ❑ Day Use Area

Notes:

Get the Facts

- ❑ Phone   276-445-3065
- ❑ Park Hours

  _____

- ❑ Reservations? _____Y _____N

  date made_____

- ❑ Open all year _____Y_____N

  dates_____

- ❑ Check in time _____
- ❑ Check out time _____
- ❑ Pet friendly _____Y _____N
- ❑ Max RV length _____
- ❑ Distance from home

  miles: _____

  hours: _____

- ❑ Address_____

  _____

  _____

Fees:

- ❑ Day Use $ _____
- ❑ Camp Sites $ _____
- ❑ RV Sites $ _____
- ❑ Refund policy

  _____

  _____

  _____

Make It Personal

Trip dates: _____ | The weather was: Sunny Cloudy Rainy Stormy Snowy Foggy Warm Cold

Why I went:
_____

_____

How I got there: (circle all that apply) Plane Train Car Bus Bike Hike RV MC
_____

I went with:
_____

We stayed in (space, cabin # etc):
_____

Most relaxing day:
_____

_____

Something funny:
_____

_____

Someone we met:
_____

_____

Best story told:
_____

_____

The kids liked this:
_____

_____

The best food:
_____

_____

Games played:
_____

_____

Something disappointing:
_____

_____

Next time I'll do this differently:
_____

_____

Fairy Stone State Park

City: Stuart   County: Patrick

Plan your trip: https://www.dcr.virginia.gov/state-parks/fairy-stone

Activities:

- ❑ Appalachian Trail
- ❑ Archery
- ❑ Biking
- ❑ Boating
- ❑ Camping
- ❑ Fishing
- ❑ Hiking
- ❑ Historic Sites
- ❑ Horseback Riding
- ❑ Hunting
- ❑ Photography
- ❑ Swimming
- ❑ Wildlife & Birding

Facilities:

- ❑ ADA
- ❑ Picnic sites
- ❑ Restrooms / Showers
- ❑ Trailer Access
- ❑ Visitor center
- ❑ Group Camping
- ❑ RV Camp
- ❑ Rustic Camping
- ❑ Cabins / Yurts / Bunkhouses
- ❑ Day Use Area

Notes:

Get the Facts

- ❑ Phone   276-930-2424
- ❑ Park Hours

  _____

- ❑ Reservations? _____Y _____N

  date made_____

- ❑ Open all year _____Y_____N

  dates_____

- ❑ Check in time _____
- ❑ Check out time _____
- ❑ Pet friendly _____Y _____N
- ❑ Max RV length _____
- ❑ Distance from home

  miles: _____

  hours: _____

- ❑ Address_____

  _____

  _____

Fees:

- ❑ Day Use $ _____
- ❑ Camp Sites $ _____
- ❑ RV Sites $ _____
- ❑ Refund policy

  _____

  _____

  _____

Make It Personal

Trip dates: _____ | The weather was: Sunny Cloudy Rainy Stormy Snowy Foggy Warm Cold

Why I went: _____

_____

How I got there: (circle all that apply) Plane Train Car Bus Bike Hike RV MC

I went with: _____

We stayed in (space, cabin # etc): _____

Most relaxing day: _____

_____

Something funny: _____

_____

Someone we met: _____

_____

Best story told: _____

_____

The kids liked this: _____

_____

The best food: _____

_____

Games played: _____

_____

Something disappointing: _____

_____

Next time I'll do this differently: _____

_____

Claytor Lake State Park
City: Dublin   County: Pulaski
Plan your trip: https://www.dcr.virginia.gov/state-parks/claytor-lake

Activities:

- ❑ Appalachian Trail
- ❑ Archery
- ❑ Biking
- ❑ Boating
- ❑ Camping
- ❑ Fishing
- ❑ Hiking
- ❑ Historic Sites
- ❑ Horseback Riding
- ❑ Hunting
- ❑ Photography
- ❑ Swimming

- ❑ Wildlife & Birding
- ❑
- ❑
- ❑
- ❑
- ❑
- ❑
- ❑
- ❑
- ❑

- ❑
- ❑
- ❑
- ❑
- ❑
- ❑
- ❑
- ❑
- ❑
- ❑
- ❑

Facilities:

- ❑ ADA
- ❑ Picnic sites
- ❑ Restrooms / Showers
- ❑ Trailer Access
- ❑ Visitor center
- ❑ Group Camping
- ❑ RV Camp
- ❑ Rustic Camping
- ❑ Cabins / Yurts / Bunkhouses
- ❑ Day Use Area

Notes:

Get the Facts

- ❑ Phone   540-643-2500
- ❑ Park Hours

  _____

- ❑ Reservations? ____Y ____N

  date made_____

- ❑ Open all year ____Y____N

  dates_____

- ❑ Check in time _____
- ❑ Check out time _____
- ❑ Pet friendly _____Y _____N
- ❑ Max RV length _____
- ❑ Distance from home

  miles: _____

  hours: _____

- ❑ Address_____

  _____

  _____

Fees:

- ❑ Day Use $ _____
- ❑ Camp Sites $ _____
- ❑ RV Sites $ _____
- ❑ Refund policy

  _____

  _____

  _____

Make It Personal

Trip dates: _____ | The weather was: Sunny Cloudy Rainy Stormy Snowy Foggy Warm Cold

Why I went:

_____

How I got there: (circle all that apply) Plane Train Car Bus Bike Hike RV MC

I went with:

We stayed in (space, cabin # etc):

Most relaxing day:

_____

Something funny:

_____

Someone we met:

_____

Best story told:

_____

The kids liked this:

_____

The best food:

_____

Games played:

_____

Something disappointing:

_____

Next time I'll do this differently:

_____

Natural Tunnel State Park
City: Duffield   County: Scott
Plan your trip: https://www.dcr.virginia.gov/state-parks/natural-tunnel

Activities:

- ❏ Appalachian Trail
- ❏ Archery
- ❏ Biking
- ❏ Boating
- ❏ Camping
- ❏ Fishing
- ❏ Hiking
- ❏ Historic Sites
- ❏ Horseback Riding
- ❏ Hunting
- ❏ Photography
- ❏ Swimming

- ❏ Wildlife & Birding
- ❏
- ❏
- ❏
- ❏
- ❏
- ❏
- ❏
- ❏
- ❏

Facilities:

- ❏ ADA
- ❏ Picnic sites
- ❏ Restrooms / Showers
- ❏ Trailer Access
- ❏ Visitor center
- ❏ Group Camping
- ❏ RV Camp
- ❏ Rustic Camping
- ❏ Cabins / Yurts / Bunkhouses
- ❏ Day Use Area

Notes:

Get the Facts

- ❏ Phone   276-940-2674
- ❏ Park Hours

  _____

- ❏ Reservations? _____Y _____N

  date made_____

- ❏ Open all year _____Y_____N

  dates_____

- ❏ Check in time _____
- ❏ Check out time _____
- ❏ Pet friendly _____Y _____N
- ❏ Max RV length _____
- ❏ Distance from home

  miles: _____

  hours: _____

- ❏ Address_____

  _____

  _____

Fees:

- ❏ Day Use $ _____
- ❏ Camp Sites $ _____
- ❏ RV Sites $ _____
- ❏ Refund policy

  _____

  _____

  _____

Make It Personal

Trip dates: | The weather was: Sunny Cloudy Rainy Stormy Snowy Foggy Warm Cold

Why I went:

How I got there: (circle all that apply) Plane Train Car Bus Bike Hike RV MC

I went with:

We stayed in (space, cabin # etc):

Most relaxing day:

Something funny:

Someone we met:

Best story told:

The kids liked this:

The best food:

Games played:

Something disappointing:

Next time I'll do this differently:

Hungry Mother State Park
City: Marion   County: Smyth

Plan your trip: https://www.dcr.virginia.gov/state-parks/hungry-mother

Activities:

- ☐ Appalachian Trail
- ☐ Archery
- ☐ Biking
- ☐ Boating
- ☐ Camping
- ☐ Fishing
- ☐ Hiking
- ☐ Historic Sites
- ☐ Horseback Riding
- ☐ Hunting
- ☐ Photography
- ☐ Swimming
- ☐ Wildlife & Birding
- ☐
- ☐
- ☐
- ☐
- ☐
- ☐
- ☐
- ☐
- ☐
- ☐
- ☐
- ☐
- ☐
- ☐
- ☐
- ☐
- ☐
- ☐
- ☐

Facilities:

- ☐ ADA
- ☐ Picnic sites
- ☐ Restrooms / Showers
- ☐ Trailer Access
- ☐ Visitor center
- ☐ Group Camping
- ☐ RV Camp
- ☐ Rustic Camping
- ☐ Cabins / Yurts / Bunkhouses
- ☐ Day Use Area

Notes:

Get the Facts

- ☐ Phone   276-781-7400
- ☐ Park Hours

  _____

- ☐ Reservations? ____Y ____N

  date made_____

- ☐ Open all year ____Y_____N

  dates_____

- ☐ Check in time _____
- ☐ Check out time _____
- ☐ Pet friendly _____Y _____N
- ☐ Max RV length _____
- ☐ Distance from home

  miles: _____

  hours: _____

- ☐ Address_____

  _____

  _____

Fees:

- ☐ Day Use $ _____
- ☐ Camp Sites $ _____
- ☐ RV Sites $ _____
- ☐ Refund policy

  _____

  _____

  _____

Make It Personal

Trip dates: _____ | The weather was: Sunny Cloudy Rainy Stormy Snowy Foggy Warm Cold

Why I went: _____

_____

How I got there: (circle all that apply) Plane Train Car Bus Bike Hike RV MC

I went with: _____

We stayed in (space, cabin # etc): _____

Most relaxing day: _____

_____

Something funny: _____

_____

Someone we met: _____

_____

Best story told: _____

_____

The kids liked this: _____

_____

The best food: _____

_____

Games played: _____

_____

Something disappointing: _____

_____

Next time I'll do this differently: _____

_____

Raccoon Branch Wilderness

City: Sugar Grove   County: Smyth

Plan your trip: http://www.vawilderness.org/raccoon-branch-wilderness.html

Activities:

- ☐ Appalachian Trail
- ☐ Archery
- ☐ Biking
- ☐ Boating
- ☐ Camping
- ☐ Fishing
- ☐ Hiking
- ☐ Historic Sites
- ☐ Horseback Riding
- ☐ Hunting
- ☐ Photography
- ☐ Swimming
- ☐ Wildlife & Birding

Facilities:

- ☐ ADA
- ☐ Picnic sites
- ☐ Restrooms / Showers
- ☐ Trailer Access
- ☐ Visitor center
- ☐ Group Camping
- ☐ RV Camp
- ☐ Rustic Camping
- ☐ Cabins / Yurts / Bunkhouses
- ☐ Day Use Area

Notes:

Get the Facts

- ☐ Phone   540-464-1661
- ☐ Park Hours

  _____

- ☐ Reservations? ____Y ____N

  date made_____

- ☐ Open all year ____Y____N

  dates_____

- ☐ Check in time _____
- ☐ Check out time _____
- ☐ Pet friendly ____Y ____N
- ☐ Max RV length _____
- ☐ Distance from home

  miles: _____

  hours: _____

- ☐ Address_____

  _____

  _____

Fees:

- ☐ Day Use $ _____
- ☐ Camp Sites $ _____
- ☐ RV Sites $ _____
- ☐ Refund policy

  _____

  _____

  _____

Make It Personal

Trip dates: _____ | The weather was: Sunny Cloudy Rainy Stormy Snowy Foggy Warm Cold

Why I went: _____

_____

How I got there: (circle all that apply) Plane Train Car Bus Bike Hike RV MC

I went with: _____

We stayed in (space, cabin # etc): _____

Most relaxing day: _____

_____

Something funny: _____

_____

Someone we met: _____

_____

Best story told: _____

_____

The kids liked this: _____

_____

The best food: _____

_____

Games played: _____

_____

Something disappointing: _____

_____

Next time I'll do this differently: _____

_____

Little Wilson Creek Wilderness
City: Abingdon   County: Washington

Plan your trip: http://www.vawilderness.org/little-wilson-creek-wilderness.html

Activities:

- ❑ Appalachian Trail
- ❑ Archery
- ❑ Biking
- ❑ Boating
- ❑ Camping
- ❑ Fishing
- ❑ Hiking
- ❑ Historic Sites
- ❑ Horseback Riding
- ❑ Hunting
- ❑ Photography
- ❑ Swimming
- ❑ Wildlife & Birding
- ❑
- ❑
- ❑
- ❑
- ❑
- ❑
- ❑
- ❑
- ❑
- ❑
- ❑
- ❑
- ❑
- ❑
- ❑
- ❑
- ❑
- ❑
- ❑
- ❑

Facilities:

- ❑ ADA
- ❑ Picnic sites
- ❑ Restrooms / Showers
- ❑ Trailer Access
- ❑ Visitor center
- ❑ Group Camping
- ❑ RV Camp
- ❑ Rustic Camping
- ❑ Cabins / Yurts / Bunkhouses
- ❑ Day Use Area

Notes:

Get the Facts

- ❑ Phone   540-464-1661
- ❑ Park Hours

    _____

- ❑ Reservations? ____Y ____N

    date made_____

- ❑ Open all year ____Y_____N

    dates_____

- ❑ Check in time _____
- ❑ Check out time _____
- ❑ Pet friendly _____Y _____N
- ❑ Max RV length _____
- ❑ Distance from home

    miles: _____

    hours: _____

- ❑ Address_____

    _____

    _____

Fees:

- ❑ Day Use $ _____
- ❑ Camp Sites $ _____
- ❑ RV Sites $ _____
- ❑ Refund policy

    _____

    _____

    _____

Make It Personal

Trip dates: _____ | The weather was: Sunny Cloudy Rainy Stormy Snowy Foggy Warm Cold

Why I went:
_____

_____

How I got there: (circle all that apply)   Plane   Train   Car   Bus   Bike   Hike   RV   MC
_____

I went with:
_____

We stayed in (space, cabin # etc):
_____

Most relaxing day:
_____

_____

Something funny:
_____

_____

Someone we met:
_____

_____

Best story told:
_____

_____

The kids liked this:
_____

_____

The best food:
_____

_____

Games played:
_____

_____

Something disappointing:
_____

_____

Next time I'll do this differently:
_____

_____

Southwest Virginia Museum HSP
City: Big Stone Gap   County: Wise

Plan your trip: https://www.dcr.virginia.gov/state-parks/southwest-virginia-museum

Activities:

- ❑ Appalachian Trail
- ❑ Archery
- ❑ Biking
- ❑ Boating
- ❑ Camping
- ❑ Fishing
- ❑ Hiking
- ❑ Historic Sites
- ❑ Horseback Riding
- ❑ Hunting
- ❑ Photography
- ❑ Swimming

- ❑ Wildlife & Birding
- ❑
- ❑
- ❑
- ❑
- ❑
- ❑
- ❑
- ❑

- ❑
- ❑
- ❑
- ❑
- ❑
- ❑
- ❑
- ❑
- ❑
- ❑
- ❑

Facilities:

- ❑ ADA
- ❑ Picnic sites
- ❑ Restrooms / Showers
- ❑ Trailer Access
- ❑ Visitor center
- ❑ Group Camping
- ❑ RV Camp
- ❑ Rustic Camping
- ❑ Cabins / Yurts / Bunkhouses
- ❑ Day Use Area

Notes:

Get the Facts

- ❑ Phone   276-523-1322
- ❑ Park Hours

  _____

- ❑ Reservations? _____Y _____N

  date made_____

- ❑ Open all year _____Y_____N

  dates_____

- ❑ Check in time _____
- ❑ Check out time _____
- ❑ Pet friendly _____Y _____N
- ❑ Max RV length _____
- ❑ Distance from home

  miles: _____

  hours: _____

- ❑ Address_____

  _____

  _____

Fees:

- ❑ Day Use $ _____
- ❑ Camp Sites $ _____
- ❑ RV Sites $ _____
- ❑ Refund policy

  _____

  _____

  _____

Make It Personal

Trip dates: _____ | The weather was: Sunny Cloudy Rainy Stormy Snowy Foggy Warm Cold

Why I went: _____

_____

How I got there: (circle all that apply) Plane Train Car Bus Bike Hike RV MC

I went with: _____

We stayed in (space, cabin # etc): _____

Most relaxing day: _____

_____

Something funny: _____

_____

Someone we met: _____

_____

Best story told: _____

_____

The kids liked this: _____

_____

The best food: _____

_____

Games played: _____

_____

Something disappointing: _____

_____

Next time I'll do this differently: _____

_____

New River Trail State Park
City: Max Meadows   County: Wythe

Plan your trip: https://www.dcr.virginia.gov/state-parks/new-river-trail

Activities:

- ❑ Appalachian Trail
- ❑ Archery
- ❑ Biking
- ❑ Boating
- ❑ Camping
- ❑ Fishing
- ❑ Hiking
- ❑ Historic Sites
- ❑ Horseback Riding
- ❑ Hunting
- ❑ Photography
- ❑ Swimming

- ❑ Wildlife & Birding
- ❑
- ❑
- ❑
- ❑
- ❑
- ❑
- ❑
- ❑
- ❑
- ❑

- ❑
- ❑
- ❑
- ❑
- ❑
- ❑
- ❑
- ❑
- ❑
- ❑
- ❑
- ❑

Facilities:

- ❑ ADA
- ❑ Picnic sites
- ❑ Restrooms / Showers
- ❑ Trailer Access
- ❑ Visitor center
- ❑ Group Camping
- ❑ RV Camp
- ❑ Rustic Camping
- ❑ Cabins / Yurts / Bunkhouses
- ❑ Day Use Area

Notes:

Get the Facts

- ❑ Phone   276-699-6778
- ❑ Park Hours

  _____

- ❑ Reservations? ____Y ____N

  date made_____

- ❑ Open all year ____Y____N

  dates_____

- ❑ Check in time _____
- ❑ Check out time _____
- ❑ Pet friendly _____Y _____N
- ❑ Max RV length _____
- ❑ Distance from home

  miles: _____

  hours: _____

- ❑ Address_____

  _____

  _____

Fees:

- ❑ Day Use $ _____
- ❑ Camp Sites $ _____
- ❑ RV Sites $ _____
- ❑ Refund policy

  _____

  _____

  _____

Make It Personal

Trip dates: | The weather was: Sunny Cloudy Rainy Stormy Snowy Foggy Warm Cold

Why I went:

How I got there: (circle all that apply)   Plane   Train   Car   Bus   Bike   Hike   RV   MC

I went with:

We stayed in (space, cabin # etc):

Most relaxing day:

Something funny:

Someone we met:

Best story told:

The kids liked this:

The best food:

Games played:

Something disappointing:

Next time I'll do this differently:

Kimberling Creek Wilderness
City: Bland   County: Bland

Plan your trip: http://www.vawilderness.org/kimberling-creek-wilderness.html

Activities:

- ❑ Appalachian Trail
- ❑ Biking
- ❑ Boating
- ❑ Fishing
- ❑ Hiking
- ❑ Horseback Riding
- ❑ Wildlife Viewing
- ❑
- ❑
- ❑
- ❑

❑ ❑ ❑ ❑ ❑ ❑ ❑ ❑ ❑ ❑ ❑

Facilities:

- ❑ ADA
- ❑ Gift Shop
- ❑ Museum
- ❑ Visitor Center
- ❑ Picnic sites
- ❑ Restrooms

❑ ❑ ❑ ❑ ❑ ❑

Our Visit:

Get the Facts

- ❑ Phone   540-464-1661
- ❑ Park Hours

  _____

- ❑ Reservations? ____Y ____N

  date made_____
- ❑ Open all year? ____Y____N

  dates_____
- ❑ Dog friendly _____Y _____N
- ❑ Distance from home

  miles: _____

  hours: _____
- ❑ Address_____

  _____

  _____

Fees:

- ❑ Day Use $ _____
- ❑ Refund policy

  _____

  _____

  _____

Notes:

Mountain Lake Wilderness

City: Newport   **County: Giles**

Plan your trip: http://www.vawilderness.org/mountain-lake-wilderness.html

Activities:

- ❑ Appalachian Trail   ❑
- ❑ Biking   ❑
- ❑ Boating   ❑
- ❑ Fishing   ❑
- ❑ Hiking   ❑
- ❑ Horseback Riding   ❑
- ❑ Wildlife Viewing   ❑
- ❑   ❑
- ❑   ❑
- ❑   ❑
- ❑   ❑

Facilities:

- ❑ ADA   ❑
- ❑ Gift Shop   ❑
- ❑ Museum   ❑
- ❑ Visitor Center   ❑
- ❑ Picnic sites   ❑
- ❑ Restrooms   ❑

Our Visit:

Get the Facts

- ❑ Phone   540-464-1661
- ❑ Park Hours

  _____

- ❑ Reservations? ____Y ____N

  date made_____

- ❑ Open all year? ____Y____N

  dates_____

- ❑ Dog friendly _____Y _____N

- ❑ Distance from home

  miles: _____

  hours: _____

- ❑ Address_____

  _____

  _____

Fees:

- ❑ Day Use $ _____
- ❑ Refund policy

  _____

  _____

  _____

Notes:

145

Peters Mountain Wilderness
City: Ripplemead   County: Giles

Plan your trip: http://www.vawilderness.org/peters-mountain-wilderness.html

Activities:

- ☐ Appalachian Trail   ☐
- ☐ Biking   ☐
- ☐ Boating   ☐
- ☐ Fishing   ☐
- ☐ Hiking   ☐
- ☐ Horseback Riding   ☐
- ☐ Wildlife Viewing   ☐
- ☐   ☐
- ☐   ☐
- ☐   ☐
- ☐   ☐

Facilities:

- ☐ ADA   ☐
- ☐ Gift Shop   ☐
- ☐ Museum   ☐
- ☐ Visitor Center   ☐
- ☐ Picnic sites   ☐
- ☐ Restrooms   ☐

Our Visit:

Get the Facts

- ☐ Phone   540-464-1661
- ☐ Park Hours

  _____

- ☐ Reservations? _____Y _____N

  date made_____

- ☐ Open all year? _____Y_____N

  dates_____

- ☐ Dog friendly _____Y _____N

- ☐ Distance from home

  miles: _____

  hours: _____

- ☐ Address_____

  _____

  _____

Fees:

- ☐ Day Use $ _____
- ☐ Refund policy

  _____

  _____

  _____

Notes:

Stone Mountain Wilderness

City: Dryden   County: Lee

Plan your trip: http://www.vawilderness.org/stone-mountain-wilderness.html

Activities:

- ❑ Appalachian Trail   ❑
- ❑ Biking   ❑
- ❑ Boating   ❑
- ❑ Fishing   ❑
- ❑ Hiking   ❑
- ❑ Horseback Riding   ❑
- ❑ Wildlife Viewing   ❑
- ❑   ❑
- ❑   ❑
- ❑   ❑
- ❑   ❑

Facilities:

- ❑ ADA   ❑
- ❑ Gift Shop   ❑
- ❑ Museum   ❑
- ❑ Visitor Center   ❑
- ❑ Picnic sites   ❑
- ❑ Restrooms   ❑

Our Visit:

Get the Facts

- ❑ Phone   540-464-1661
- ❑ Park Hours

  _____

- ❑ Reservations? _____Y _____N

  date made_____

- ❑ Open all year? _____Y _____N

  dates_____

- ❑ Dog friendly _____Y _____N

- ❑ Distance from home

  miles: _____

  hours: _____

- ❑ Address_____

  _____

  _____

Fees:

- ❑ Day Use $ _____
- ❑ Refund policy

  _____

  _____

  _____

Notes:

Brush Mountain Wilderness

City: Blacksburg   County: Montgomery

Plan your trip: http://www.vawilderness.org/va-wilderness.html

Activities:

- ❑ Appalachian Trail   ❑
- ❑ Biking   ❑
- ❑ Boating   ❑
- ❑ Fishing   ❑
- ❑ Hiking   ❑
- ❑ Horseback Riding   ❑
- ❑ Wildlife Viewing   ❑
- ❑   ❑
- ❑   ❑
- ❑   ❑
- ❑   ❑

Facilities:

- ❑ ADA   ❑
- ❑ Gift Shop   ❑
- ❑ Museum   ❑
- ❑ Visitor Center   ❑
- ❑ Picnic sites   ❑
- ❑ Restrooms   ❑

Our Visit:

Get the Facts

- ❑ Phone   540-464-1661
- ❑ Park Hours

  _____

- ❑ Reservations? ____Y ____N

  date made_____

- ❑ Open all year? ____Y____N

  dates_____

- ❑ Dog friendly _____Y _____N

- ❑ Distance from home

  miles: _____

  hours: _____

- ❑ Address_____

  _____

  _____

Fees:

- ❑ Day Use $ _____
- ❑ Refund policy

  _____

  _____

  _____

Notes:

Brush Mountain East Wilderness
City: McDonalds Mill   County: Montgomery

Plan your trip: http://www.vawilderness.org/brush-mountain-east-wilderness.html

Activities:

- ❑ Appalachian Trail   ❑
- ❑ Biking   ❑
- ❑ Boating   ❑
- ❑ Fishing   ❑
- ❑ Hiking   ❑
- ❑ Horseback Riding   ❑
- ❑ Wildlife Viewing   ❑
- ❑   ❑
- ❑   ❑
- ❑   ❑
- ❑   ❑

Facilities:

- ❑ ADA   ❑
- ❑ Gift Shop   ❑
- ❑ Museum   ❑
- ❑ Visitor Center   ❑
- ❑ Picnic sites   ❑
- ❑ Restrooms   ❑

Our Visit:

Get the Facts

- ❑ Phone   540-464-1661
- ❑ Park Hours

  _____

- ❑ Reservations? ____Y ____N

  date made_____

- ❑ Open all year? ____Y____N

  dates_____

- ❑ Dog friendly _____Y _____N

- ❑ Distance from home

  miles: _____

  hours: _____

- ❑ Address_____

  _____

  _____

Fees:

- ❑ Day Use $ _____
- ❑ Refund policy

  _____

  _____

  _____

Notes:

Garden Mountain Wilderness
City: Burkes Garden   County: Tazewell

Plan your trip: www.vawilderness.org/garden-mountain-wilderness.html

Activities:

- ❏ Appalachian Trail ❏
- ❏ Biking ❏
- ❏ Boating ❏
- ❏ Fishing ❏
- ❏ Hiking ❏
- ❏ Horseback Riding ❏
- ❏ Wildlife Viewing ❏
- ❏ ❏
- ❏ ❏
- ❏ ❏
- ❏ ❏

Facilities:

- ❏ ADA ❏
- ❏ Gift Shop ❏
- ❏ Museum ❏
- ❏ Visitor Center ❏
- ❏ Picnic sites ❏
- ❏ Restrooms ❏

Our Visit:

Get the Facts

- ❏ Phone   540-464-1661
- ❏ Park Hours

    _____

- ❏ Reservations? ____Y ____N

    date made_____

- ❏ Open all year? ____Y____N

    dates_____

- ❏ Dog friendly _____Y _____N

- ❏ Distance from home

    miles: _____

    hours: _____

- ❏ Address_____

    _____

    _____

Fees:

- ❏ Day Use $ _____
- ❏ Refund policy

    _____

    _____

    _____

Notes:

Beartown Wilderness

City: Tazewell   County: Tazewell

Plan your trip: http://www.vawilderness.org/beartown-wilderness.html

Activities:

- ❑ Appalachian Trail   ❑
- ❑ Biking   ❑
- ❑ Boating   ❑
- ❑ Fishing   ❑
- ❑ Hiking   ❑
- ❑ Horseback Riding   ❑
- ❑ Wildlife Viewing   ❑
- ❑   ❑
- ❑   ❑
- ❑   ❑
- ❑   ❑

Facilities:

- ❑ ADA   ❑
- ❑ Gift Shop   ❑
- ❑ Museum   ❑
- ❑ Visitor Center   ❑
- ❑ Picnic sites   ❑
- ❑ Restrooms   ❑

Our Visit:

Get the Facts

- ❑ Phone   540-464-1661
- ❑ Park Hours

  _____

- ❑ Reservations? _____ Y _____ N

  date made_____

- ❑ Open all year? _____ Y_____ N

  dates_____

- ❑ Dog friendly _____ Y _____ N

- ❑ Distance from home

  miles: _____

  hours: _____

- ❑ Address_____

  _____

  _____

Fees:

- ❑ Day Use $ _____
- ❑ Refund policy

  _____

  _____

  _____

Notes:

Hunting Camp Creek Wilderness

City: Tazewell   **County: Tazewell**

Plan your trip: http://www.vawilderness.org/hunting-camp-creek-wilderness.html

Activities:

- ☐ Appalachian Trail   ☐
- ☐ Biking   ☐
- ☐ Boating   ☐
- ☐ Fishing   ☐
- ☐ Hiking   ☐
- ☐ Horseback Riding   ☐
- ☐ Wildlife Viewing   ☐
- ☐   ☐
- ☐   ☐
- ☐   ☐
- ☐   ☐

Facilities:

- ☐ ADA   ☐
- ☐ Gift Shop   ☐
- ☐ Museum   ☐
- ☐ Visitor Center   ☐
- ☐ Picnic sites   ☐
- ☐ Restrooms   ☐

Our Visit:

Get the Facts

- ☐ Phone   540-464-1661
- ☐ Park Hours

  _____

- ☐ Reservations? _____Y _____N

  date made_____

- ☐ Open all year? _____Y_____N

  dates_____

- ☐ Dog friendly _____Y _____N

- ☐ Distance from home

  miles: _____

  hours: _____

- ☐ Address_____

  _____

  _____

Fees:

- ☐ Day Use $ _____
- ☐ Refund policy

  _____

  _____

  _____

Notes:

Shot Tower State Park
City: Max Meadows   County: Wythe

Plan your trip: https://www.dcr.virginia.gov/state-parks/shot-tower

Activities:

- ❏ Appalachian Trail   ❏
- ❏ Biking   ❏
- ❏ Boating   ❏
- ❏ Fishing   ❏
- ❏ Hiking   ❏
- ❏ Horseback Riding   ❏
- ❏ Wildlife Viewing   ❏
- ❏   ❏
- ❏   ❏
- ❏   ❏
- ❏   ❏

Facilities:

- ❏ ADA   ❏
- ❏ Gift Shop   ❏
- ❏ Museum   ❏
- ❏ Visitor Center   ❏
- ❏ Picnic sites   ❏
- ❏ Restrooms   ❏

Our Visit:

Get the Facts

- ❏ Phone   276-699-6778
- ❏ Park Hours

  _____

- ❏ Reservations? _____Y _____N

  date made_____

- ❏ Open all year? _____Y_____N

  dates_____

- ❏ Dog friendly _____Y _____N

- ❏ Distance from home

  miles: _____

  hours: _____

- ❏ Address_____

  _____

  _____

Fees:

- ❏ Day Use $ _____
- ❏ Refund policy

  _____

  _____

  _____

Notes:

Little Dry Run Wilderness
City: Speedwell   County: Wythe

Plan your trip: http://www.vawilderness.org/little-dry-run-wilderness.html

Activities:

- ❑ Appalachian Trail
- ❑ Biking
- ❑ Boating
- ❑ Fishing
- ❑ Hiking
- ❑ Horseback Riding
- ❑ Wildlife Viewing
- ❑
- ❑
- ❑
- ❑

❑ ❑ ❑ ❑ ❑ ❑ ❑ ❑ ❑ ❑ ❑

Facilities:

- ❑ ADA
- ❑ Gift Shop
- ❑ Museum
- ❑ Visitor Center
- ❑ Picnic sites
- ❑ Restrooms

❑ ❑ ❑ ❑ ❑ ❑

Our Visit:

Get the Facts

- ❑ Phone   540-464-1661
- ❑ Park Hours

  _____

- ❑ Reservations? ____Y ____N

  date made_____

- ❑ Open all year? ____Y____N

  dates_____

- ❑ Dog friendly _____Y _____N

- ❑ Distance from home

  miles: _____

  hours: _____

- ❑ Address_____

  _____

  _____

Fees:

- ❑ Day Use $ _____
- ❑ Refund policy

  _____

  _____

  _____

Notes:

Notes:

Historic Saltville

City: Saltville   County: Smyth

Plan your trip: https://www.saltville.org/?q=node/2

History:

Get the Facts

- ❏ Address_____
  _____
- ❏ Phone   540-496-5342
- ❏ Best season to visit
  _____
- ❏ Pet Friendly   Y   N
- ❏ Reservations?   Y   N
  date made_____
- ❏ Distance from home
  miles: _____
  hours: _____

Things To Do:

- ❏ ADA availability
- ❏ Public Restrooms
- ❏ Gift Shop
- ❏ Museum
- ❏ Visitor Center
- ❏ Picnic areas
- ❏ Chamber of Commerce
- ❏ Monuments
- ❏ Art Galleries
- ❏ Tours
- ❏ Street Art
- ❏ Natural Areas
- ❏ Living History
- ❏ Cemetery
- ❏ Amphitheater

Places I Want to Visit in the Area:

Restaurants:

Boutiques & Shops:

Monuments:

Museums:

Budget for this trip:

Parking	$
Food	$
Museums	$
Hotel	$
Shopping	$
Total	$

Notes:

Restaurant:

My Experience:

Shopping:

Best Find:

The shop I want to go back to:

Museum:

The coolest thing I learned about this area:

Other:

Abingdon Historic District

City: Abingdon   **County: Washington**

Plan your trip: https://www.virginia.org/listings/HistoricSites/AbingdonHistoricDistrict/

History:

Things To Do:

- ❑ ADA availability
- ❑ Public Restrooms
- ❑ Gift Shop
- ❑ Museum
- ❑ Visitor Center
- ❑ Picnic areas
- ❑ Chamber of Commerce
- ❑ Monuments
- ❑ Art Galleries
- ❑ Tours
- ❑ Street Art
- ❑ Natural Areas
- ❑ Living History
- ❑ Cemetery
- ❑ Amphitheater

Places I Want to Visit in the Area:

Restaurants:
Boutiques & Shops:
Monuments:
Museums:

Get the Facts

- ❑ Address_____
  _____
- ❑ Phone   800-435-3440
- ❑ Best season to visit
  _____
- ❑ Pet Friendly   Y   N
- ❑ Reservations?   Y   N
  date made_____
- ❑ Distance from home
  miles: _____
  hours: _____

Budget for this trip:

Parking	$
Food	$
Museums	$
Hotel	$
Shopping	$
Total	$

Notes:

Restaurant:

My Experience:

Shopping:

Best Find:

The shop I want to go back to:

Museum:

The coolest thing I learned about this area:

Other:

Notes:

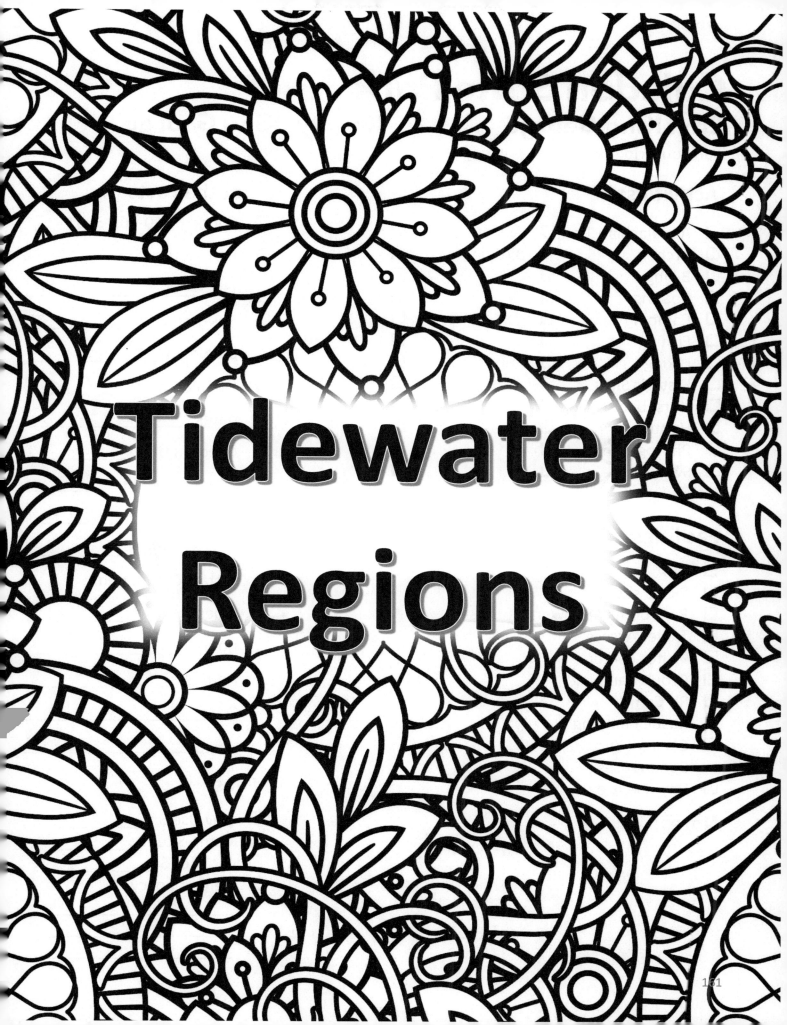

Caledon State Park

City: King George   **County: King George**

Plan your trip: https://www.dcr.virginia.gov/state-parks/caledon

Activities:

- ❑ Appalachian Trail
- ❑ Archery
- ❑ Biking
- ❑ Boating
- ❑ Camping
- ❑ Fishing
- ❑ Hiking
- ❑ Historic Sites
- ❑ Horseback Riding
- ❑ Hunting
- ❑ Photography
- ❑ Swimming
- ❑ Wildlife & Birding

Facilities:

- ❑ ADA
- ❑ Picnic sites
- ❑ Restrooms / Showers
- ❑ Trailer Access
- ❑ Visitor center
- ❑ Group Camping
- ❑ RV Camp
- ❑ Rustic Camping
- ❑ Cabins / Yurts / Bunkhouses
- ❑ Day Use Area

Notes:

Get the Facts

- ❑ Phone   540-663-3861
- ❑ Park Hours

  _____

- ❑ Reservations? _____Y _____N

  date made_____

- ❑ Open all year _____Y_____N

  dates_____

- ❑ Check in time _____
- ❑ Check out time _____
- ❑ Pet friendly _____Y _____N
- ❑ Max RV length _____
- ❑ Distance from home

  miles: _____

  hours: _____

- ❑ Address_____

  _____

  _____

Fees:

- ❑ Day Use $ _____
- ❑ Camp Sites $ _____
- ❑ RV Sites $ _____
- ❑ Refund policy

  _____

  _____

  _____

Make It Personal

Trip dates: _____

The weather was: Sunny Cloudy Rainy Stormy Snowy Foggy Warm Cold

Why I went: _____

How I got there: (circle all that apply) Plane Train Car Bus Bike Hike RV MC

I went with: _____

We stayed in (space, cabin # etc): _____

Most relaxing day: _____

Something funny: _____

Someone we met: _____

Best story told: _____

The kids liked this: _____

The best food: _____

Games played: _____

Something disappointing: _____

Next time I'll do this differently: _____

Belle Isle State Park

City: Lancaster   **County: Lancaster**

Plan your trip: https://www.dcr.virginia.gov/state-parks/belle-isle

Activities:

- ❑ Appalachian Trail
- ❑ Archery
- ❑ Biking
- ❑ Boating
- ❑ Camping
- ❑ Fishing
- ❑ Hiking
- ❑ Historic Sites
- ❑ Horseback Riding
- ❑ Hunting
- ❑ Photography
- ❑ Swimming
- ❑ Wildlife & Birding

Facilities:

- ❑ ADA
- ❑ Picnic sites
- ❑ Restrooms / Showers
- ❑ Trailer Access
- ❑ Visitor center
- ❑ Group Camping
- ❑ RV Camp
- ❑ Rustic Camping
- ❑ Cabins / Yurts / Bunkhouses
- ❑ Day Use Area

Notes:

Get the Facts

- ❑ Phone   804-462-5030
- ❑ Park Hours

  _____

- ❑ Reservations? _____Y _____N

  date made_____

- ❑ Open all year _____Y_____N

  dates_____

- ❑ Check in time _____
- ❑ Check out time _____
- ❑ Pet friendly _____Y _____N
- ❑ Max RV length _____
- ❑ Distance from home

  miles: _____

  hours: _____

- ❑ Address_____

  _____

  _____

Fees:

- ❑ Day Use $ _____
- ❑ Camp Sites $ _____
- ❑ RV Sites $ _____
- ❑ Refund policy

  _____

  _____

  _____

Make It Personal

Trip dates: _____ | The weather was: Sunny   Cloudy   Rainy   Stormy   Snowy   Foggy   Warm   Cold

Why I went:
_____

How I got there: (circle all that apply)   Plane   Train   Car   Bus   Bike   Hike   RV   MC

I went with:
_____

We stayed in (space, cabin # etc):
_____

Most relaxing day:
_____

Something funny:
_____

Someone we met:
_____

Best story told:
_____

The kids liked this:
_____

The best food:
_____

Games played:
_____

Something disappointing:
_____

Next time I'll do this differently:
_____

Chippokes Plantation State Park

City: Surry   **County: Surry**

Plan your trip: https://www.dcr.virginia.gov/state-parks/chippokes-plantation

Activities:

- ❑ Appalachian Trail
- ❑ Archery
- ❑ Biking
- ❑ Boating
- ❑ Camping
- ❑ Fishing
- ❑ Hiking
- ❑ Historic Sites
- ❑ Horseback Riding
- ❑ Hunting
- ❑ Photography
- ❑ Swimming
- ❑ Wildlife & Birding
- ❑
- ❑
- ❑
- ❑
- ❑
- ❑
- ❑

Facilities:

- ❑ ADA
- ❑ Picnic sites
- ❑ Restrooms / Showers
- ❑ Trailer Access
- ❑ Visitor center
- ❑ Group Camping
- ❑ RV Camp
- ❑ Rustic Camping
- ❑ Cabins / Yurts / Bunkhouses
- ❑ Day Use Area

Notes:

Get the Facts

- ❑ Phone   757-294-3728
- ❑ Park Hours

  _____

- ❑ Reservations? ____Y ____N

  date made_____

- ❑ Open all year ____Y____N

  dates_____

- ❑ Check in time _____
- ❑ Check out time _____
- ❑ Pet friendly _____Y _____N
- ❑ Max RV length _____
- ❑ Distance from home

  miles: _____

  hours: _____

- ❑ Address_____

  _____

  _____

Fees:

- ❑ Day Use $ _____
- ❑ Camp Sites $ _____
- ❑ RV Sites $ _____
- ❑ Refund policy

  _____

  _____

  _____

Make It Personal

Trip dates: _____ | The weather was: Sunny Cloudy Rainy Stormy Snowy Foggy Warm Cold

Why I went: _____

_____

How I got there: (circle all that apply)   Plane   Train   Car   Bus   Bike   Hike   RV   MC

I went with: _____

We stayed in (space, cabin # etc): _____

Most relaxing day: _____

_____

Something funny: _____

_____

Someone we met: _____

_____

Best story told: _____

_____

The kids liked this: _____

_____

The best food: _____

_____

Games played: _____

_____

Something disappointing: _____

_____

Next time I'll do this differently: _____

_____

False Cape State Park
City: Virginia Beach   County: Virginia Beach

Plan your trip: https://www.dcr.virginia.gov/state-parks/false-cape

Activities:

- ❑ Appalachian Trail
- ❑ Archery
- ❑ Biking
- ❑ Boating
- ❑ Camping
- ❑ Fishing
- ❑ Hiking
- ❑ Historic Sites
- ❑ Horseback Riding
- ❑ Hunting
- ❑ Photography
- ❑ Swimming
- ❑ Wildlife & Birding
- ❑
- ❑
- ❑
- ❑
- ❑
- ❑
- ❑
- ❑
- ❑
- ❑
- ❑
- ❑
- ❑
- ❑
- ❑
- ❑
- ❑
- ❑

Facilities:

- ❑ ADA
- ❑ Picnic sites
- ❑ Restrooms / Showers
- ❑ Trailer Access
- ❑ Visitor center
- ❑ Group Camping
- ❑ RV Camp
- ❑ Rustic Camping
- ❑ Cabins / Yurts / Bunkhouses
- ❑ Day Use Area

Notes:

Get the Facts

- ❑ Phone   757-426-7128
- ❑ Park Hours

  _____

- ❑ Reservations? _____Y _____N

  date made_____

- ❑ Open all year _____Y_____N

  dates_____

- ❑ Check in time _____
- ❑ Check out time _____
- ❑ Pet friendly _____Y _____N
- ❑ Max RV length _____
- ❑ Distance from home

  miles: _____

  hours: _____

- ❑ Address_____

  _____

  _____

Fees:

- ❑ Day Use $ _____
- ❑ Camp Sites $ _____
- ❑ RV Sites $ _____
- ❑ Refund policy

  _____

  _____

  _____

Make It Personal

Trip dates: _____

The weather was: Sunny Cloudy Rainy Stormy Snowy Foggy Warm Cold

Why I went: _____

How I got there: (circle all that apply) Plane Train Car Bus Bike Hike RV MC

I went with: _____

We stayed in (space, cabin # etc): _____

Most relaxing day: _____

Something funny: _____

Someone we met: _____

Best story told: _____

The kids liked this: _____

The best food: _____

Games played: _____

Something disappointing: _____

Next time I'll do this differently: _____

First Landing State Park
City: Virginia Beach   County: Virginia Beach

Plan your trip: https://www.dcr.virginia.gov/state-parks/first-landing

Activities:

- ❑ Appalachian Trail
- ❑ Archery
- ❑ Biking
- ❑ Boating
- ❑ Camping
- ❑ Fishing
- ❑ Hiking
- ❑ Historic Sites
- ❑ Horseback Riding
- ❑ Hunting
- ❑ Photography
- ❑ Swimming
- ❑ Wildlife & Birding
- ❑
- ❑
- ❑
- ❑
- ❑
- ❑
- ❑
- ❑
- ❑
- ❑
- ❑
- ❑
- ❑
- ❑
- ❑
- ❑
- ❑
- ❑
- ❑
- ❑
- ❑
- ❑

Facilities:

- ❑ ADA
- ❑ Picnic sites
- ❑ Restrooms / Showers
- ❑ Trailer Access
- ❑ Visitor center
- ❑ Group Camping
- ❑ RV Camp
- ❑ Rustic Camping
- ❑ Cabins / Yurts / Bunkhouses
- ❑ Day Use Area

Notes:

Get the Facts

- ❑ Phone   757-412-2300
- ❑ Park Hours

  _____

- ❑ Reservations? ____Y ____N

  date made_____

- ❑ Open all year ____Y____N

  dates_____

- ❑ Check in time _____
- ❑ Check out time _____
- ❑ Pet friendly _____Y _____N
- ❑ Max RV length _____
- ❑ Distance from home

  miles: _____

  hours: _____

- ❑ Address_____

  _____

  _____

Fees:

- ❑ Day Use $ _____
- ❑ Camp Sites $ _____
- ❑ RV Sites $ _____
- ❑ Refund policy

  _____

  _____

  _____

Make It Personal

Trip dates: | The weather was: Sunny Cloudy Rainy Stormy Snowy Foggy Warm Cold

Why I went:

How I got there: (circle all that apply) Plane Train Car Bus Bike Hike RV MC

I went with:

We stayed in (space, cabin # etc):

Most relaxing day:

Something funny:

Someone we met:

Best story told:

The kids liked this:

The best food:

Games played:

Something disappointing:

Next time I'll do this differently:

Westmoreland State Park

City: Montross   **County: Westmoreland**

Plan your trip: https://www.dcr.virginia.gov/state-parks/westmoreland

Activities:

- ❑ Appalachian Trail
- ❑ Archery
- ❑ Biking
- ❑ Boating
- ❑ Camping
- ❑ Fishing
- ❑ Hiking
- ❑ Historic Sites
- ❑ Horseback Riding
- ❑ Hunting
- ❑ Photography
- ❑ Swimming
- ❑ Wildlife & Birding
- ❑
- ❑
- ❑
- ❑
- ❑
- ❑
- ❑
- ❑
- ❑
- ❑
- ❑
- ❑
- ❑
- ❑
- ❑
- ❑
- ❑
- ❑
- ❑
- ❑
- ❑

Facilities:

- ❑ ADA
- ❑ Picnic sites
- ❑ Restrooms / Showers
- ❑ Trailer Access
- ❑ Visitor center
- ❑ Group Camping
- ❑ RV Camp
- ❑ Rustic Camping
- ❑ Cabins / Yurts / Bunkhouses
- ❑ Day Use Area

Notes:

Get the Facts

- ❑ Phone   804-493-8821
- ❑ Park Hours

  _____

- ❑ Reservations? _____Y _____N

  date made_____

- ❑ Open all year _____Y_____N

  dates_____

- ❑ Check in time _____
- ❑ Check out time _____
- ❑ Pet friendly _____Y _____N
- ❑ Max RV length _____
- ❑ Distance from home

  miles: _____

  hours: _____

- ❑ Address_____

  _____

  _____

Fees:

- ❑ Day Use $ _____
- ❑ Camp Sites $ _____
- ❑ RV Sites $ _____
- ❑ Refund policy

  _____

  _____

  _____

Make It Personal

Trip dates:

The weather was: Sunny Cloudy Rainy Stormy Snowy Foggy Warm Cold

Why I went:

How I got there: (circle all that apply) Plane Train Car Bus Bike Hike RV MC

I went with:

We stayed in (space, cabin # etc):

Most relaxing day:

Something funny:

Someone we met:

Best story told:

The kids liked this:

The best food:

Games played:

Something disappointing:

Next time I'll do this differently:

York River State Park

City: Williamsburg   County: James City

Plan your trip: https://www.dcr.virginia.gov/state-parks/york-river

Activities:

- ❑ Appalachian Trail   ❑
- ❑ Biking   ❑
- ❑ Boating   ❑
- ❑ Fishing   ❑
- ❑ Hiking   ❑
- ❑ Horseback Riding   ❑
- ❑ Wildlife Viewing   ❑
- ❑   ❑
- ❑   ❑
- ❑   ❑
- ❑   ❑

Facilities:

- ❑ ADA   ❑
- ❑ Gift Shop   ❑
- ❑ Museum   ❑
- ❑ Visitor Center   ❑
- ❑ Picnic sites   ❑
- ❑ Restrooms   ❑

Our Visit:

Get the Facts

- ❑ Phone   757-566-3036
- ❑ Park Hours

  _____

- ❑ Reservations? _____Y _____N

  date made_____

- ❑ Open all year? _____Y_____N

  dates_____

- ❑ Dog friendly _____Y _____N

- ❑ Distance from home

  miles: _____

  hours: _____

- ❑ Address_____

  _____

  _____

Fees:

- ❑ Day Use $ _____
- ❑ Refund policy

  _____

  _____

  _____

Notes:

Notes:

Historic Jamestown

City: Jamestown   **County: James City**

Plan your trip: https://historicjamestowne.org/

History:

Things To Do:

- ❏ ADA availability
- ❏ Public Restrooms
- ❏ Gift Shop
- ❏ Museum
- ❏ Visitor Center
- ❏ Picnic areas
- ❏ Chamber of Commerce
- ❏ Monuments
- ❏ Art Galleries
- ❏ Tours
- ❏ Street Art
- ❏ Natural Areas
- ❏ Living History
- ❏ Cemetery
- ❏ Amphitheater

Places I Want to Visit in the Area:

Restaurants:
Boutiques & Shops:
Monuments:
Museums:

Get the Facts

- ❏ Address_____
  _____
- ❏ Phone   757-856-1250
- ❏ Best season to visit
  _____
- ❏ Pet Friendly   Y   N
- ❏ Reservations?   Y   N
  date made_____
- ❏ Distance from home
  miles: _____
  hours: _____

Budget for this trip:

Parking	$
Food	$
Museums	$
Hotel	$
Shopping	$
Total	$

Notes:

Restaurant:

My Experience:

Shopping:

Best Find:

The shop I want to go back to:

Museum:

The coolest thing I learned about this area:

Other:

Name:

City: County:

Plan your trip:

Activities:

- ❑ Appalachian Trail
- ❑ Archery
- ❑ Biking
- ❑ Boating
- ❑ Camping
- ❑ Fishing
- ❑ Hiking
- ❑ Historic Sites
- ❑ Horseback Riding
- ❑ Hunting
- ❑ Photography
- ❑ Swimming
- ❑ Wildlife & Birding

Facilities:

- ❑ ADA
- ❑ Picnic sites
- ❑ Restrooms / Showers
- ❑ Trailer Access
- ❑ Visitor center
- ❑ Group Camping
- ❑ RV Camp
- ❑ Rustic Camping
- ❑ Cabins / Yurts / Bunkhouses
- ❑ Day Use Area

Notes:

Get the Facts

- ❑ Phone _____
- ❑ Park Hours

  _____

- ❑ Reservations? ____Y ____N

  date made_____

- ❑ Open all year ____Y____N

  dates_____

- ❑ Check in time _____
- ❑ Check out time _____
- ❑ Pet friendly _____Y _____N
- ❑ Max RV length _____
- ❑ Distance from home

  miles: _____

  hours: _____

- ❑ Address_____

  _____

  _____

Fees:

- ❑ Day Use $ _____
- ❑ Camp Sites $ _____
- ❑ RV Sites $ _____
- ❑ Refund policy

  _____

  _____

  _____

Make It Personal

Trip dates:

The weather was: Sunny Cloudy Rainy Stormy Snowy Foggy Warm Cold

Why I went:

How I got there: (circle all that apply) Plane Train Car Bus Bike Hike RV MC

I went with:

We stayed in (space, cabin # etc):

Most relaxing day:

Something funny:

Someone we met:

Best story told:

The kids liked this:

The best food:

Games played:

Something disappointing:

Next time I'll do this differently:

Name:

City: **County:**

Plan your trip:

Activities:

- ❑ Appalachian Trail
- ❑ Archery
- ❑ Biking
- ❑ Boating
- ❑ Camping
- ❑ Fishing
- ❑ Hiking
- ❑ Historic Sites
- ❑ Horseback Riding
- ❑ Hunting
- ❑ Photography
- ❑ Swimming
- ❑ Wildlife & Birding

Facilities:

- ❑ ADA
- ❑ Picnic sites
- ❑ Restrooms / Showers
- ❑ Trailer Access
- ❑ Visitor center
- ❑ Group Camping
- ❑ RV Camp
- ❑ Rustic Camping
- ❑ Cabins / Yurts / Bunkhouses
- ❑ Day Use Area

Notes:

Get the Facts

- ❑ Phone _____
- ❑ Park Hours

  _____

- ❑ Reservations? ____Y ____N

  date made_____

- ❑ Open all year ____Y_____N

  dates_____

- ❑ Check in time _____
- ❑ Check out time _____
- ❑ Pet friendly _____Y _____N
- ❑ Max RV length _____
- ❑ Distance from home

  miles: _____

  hours: _____

- ❑ Address_____

  _____

  _____

Fees:

- ❑ Day Use $ _____
- ❑ Camp Sites $ _____
- ❑ RV Sites $ _____
- ❑ Refund policy

  _____

  _____

  _____

Make It Personal

Trip dates: _____ | The weather was: Sunny Cloudy Rainy Stormy Snowy Foggy Warm Cold

Why I went:
_____

How I got there: (circle all that apply) Plane Train Car Bus Bike Hike RV MC

I went with:
_____

We stayed in (space, cabin # etc):
_____

Most relaxing day:
_____

Something funny:
_____

Someone we met:
_____

Best story told:
_____

The kids liked this:
_____

The best food:
_____

Games played:
_____

Something disappointing:
_____

Next time I'll do this differently:
_____

Name:
City: County:
Plan your trip:

Activities:

- ☐ Appalachian Trail
- ☐ Archery
- ☐ Biking
- ☐ Boating
- ☐ Camping
- ☐ Fishing
- ☐ Hiking
- ☐ Historic Sites
- ☐ Horseback Riding
- ☐ Hunting
- ☐ Photography
- ☐ Swimming
- ☐ Wildlife & Birding

☐ ☐ ☐ ☐ ☐ ☐ ☐ ☐ ☐ ☐ ☐
☐ ☐ ☐ ☐ ☐ ☐ ☐ ☐ ☐ ☐ ☐ ☐

Facilities:

- ☐ ADA
- ☐ Picnic sites
- ☐ Restrooms / Showers
- ☐ Trailer Access
- ☐ Visitor center
- ☐ Group Camping
- ☐ RV Camp
- ☐ Rustic Camping
- ☐ Cabins / Yurts / Bunkhouses
- ☐ Day Use Area

Notes:

Get the Facts

- ☐ Phone _____
- ☐ Park Hours

  _____

- ☐ Reservations? ____Y ____N

  date made_____

- ☐ Open all year ____Y_____N

  dates_____

- ☐ Check in time _____
- ☐ Check out time _____
- ☐ Pet friendly _____Y _____N
- ☐ Max RV length _____
- ☐ Distance from home

  miles: _____

  hours: _____

- ☐ Address_____

  _____

  _____

Fees:

- ☐ Day Use $ _____
- ☐ Camp Sites $ _____
- ☐ RV Sites $ _____
- ☐ Refund policy

  _____

  _____

  _____

Make It Personal

Trip dates: _____ | The weather was: Sunny Cloudy Rainy Stormy Snowy Foggy Warm Cold

Why I went: _____

_____

How I got there: (circle all that apply) Plane   Train   Car   Bus   Bike   Hike   RV   MC

I went with: _____

We stayed in (space, cabin # etc): _____

Most relaxing day: _____

_____

Something funny: _____

_____

Someone we met: _____

_____

Best story told: _____

_____

The kids liked this: _____

_____

The best food: _____

_____

Games played: _____

_____

Something disappointing: _____

_____

Next time I'll do this differently: _____

_____

Name:

City: County:

Plan your trip:

Activities:

- ❑ Appalachian Trail   ❑
- ❑ Biking   ❑
- ❑ Boating   ❑
- ❑ Fishing   ❑
- ❑ Hiking   ❑
- ❑ Horseback Riding   ❑
- ❑ Wildlife Viewing   ❑
- ❑   ❑
- ❑   ❑
- ❑   ❑
- ❑   ❑

Facilities:

- ❑ ADA   ❑
- ❑ Gift Shop   ❑
- ❑ Museum   ❑
- ❑ Visitor Center   ❑
- ❑ Picnic sites   ❑
- ❑ Restrooms   ❑

Our Visit:

Get the Facts

- ❑ Phone_____
- ❑ Park Hours

  _____

- ❑ Reservations? ____Y ____N

  date made_____

- ❑ Open all year? ____Y____N

  dates_____

- ❑ Dog friendly _____Y _____N
- ❑ Distance from home

  miles: _____

  hours: _____

- ❑ Address_____

  _____

  _____

Fees:

- ❑ Day Use $ _____
- ❑ Refund policy

  _____

  _____

  _____

Notes:

Name:

City: County:

Plan your trip:

Activities:

- ❏ Appalachian Trail   ❏
- ❏ Biking   ❏
- ❏ Boating   ❏
- ❏ Fishing   ❏
- ❏ Hiking   ❏
- ❏ Horseback Riding   ❏
- ❏ Wildlife Viewing   ❏
- ❏   ❏
- ❏   ❏
- ❏   ❏
- ❏   ❏

Facilities:

- ❏ ADA   ❏
- ❏ Gift Shop   ❏
- ❏ Museum   ❏
- ❏ Visitor Center   ❏
- ❏ Picnic sites   ❏
- ❏ Restrooms   ❏

Our Visit:

Get the Facts

- ❏ Phone_____
- ❏ Park Hours

  _____

- ❏ Reservations? _____Y _____N

  date made_____

- ❏ Open all year? _____Y_____N

  dates_____

- ❏ Dog friendly _____Y _____N
- ❏ Distance from home

  miles: _____

  hours: _____

- ❏ Address_____

  _____

  _____

Fees:

- ❏ Day Use $ _____
- ❏ Refund policy

  _____

  _____

  _____

Notes:

Name:

City: County:

Plan your trip:

Activities:

- ❑ Appalachian Trail   ❑
- ❑ Biking   ❑
- ❑ Boating   ❑
- ❑ Fishing   ❑
- ❑ Hiking   ❑
- ❑ Horseback Riding   ❑
- ❑ Wildlife Viewing   ❑
- ❑   ❑
- ❑   ❑
- ❑   ❑
- ❑   ❑

Facilities:

- ❑ ADA   ❑
- ❑ Gift Shop   ❑
- ❑ Museum   ❑
- ❑ Visitor Center   ❑
- ❑ Picnic sites   ❑
- ❑ Restrooms   ❑

Our Visit:

Get the Facts

- ❑ Phone_____
- ❑ Park Hours

  _____

- ❑ Reservations? _____Y _____N

  date made_____

- ❑ Open all year? _____Y_____N

  dates_____

- ❑ Dog friendly _____Y _____N
- ❑ Distance from home

  miles: _____

  hours: _____

- ❑ Address_____

  _____

  _____

Fees:

- ❑ Day Use $ _____
- ❑ Refund policy

  _____

  _____

  _____

Notes:

Name:

City: ## County:

Plan your trip:

Activities:

- ❑ Appalachian Trail   ❑
- ❑ Biking   ❑
- ❑ Boating   ❑
- ❑ Fishing   ❑
- ❑ Hiking   ❑
- ❑ Horseback Riding   ❑
- ❑ Wildlife Viewing   ❑
- ❑   ❑
- ❑   ❑
- ❑   ❑
- ❑   ❑

Facilities:

- ❑ ADA   ❑
- ❑ Gift Shop   ❑
- ❑ Museum   ❑
- ❑ Visitor Center   ❑
- ❑ Picnic sites   ❑
- ❑ Restrooms   ❑

Our Visit:

Get the Facts

- ❑ Phone_____
- ❑ Park Hours

  _____

- ❑ Reservations? _____Y _____N

  date made_____

- ❑ Open all year? _____Y_____N

  dates_____

- ❑ Dog friendly _____Y _____N
- ❑ Distance from home

  miles: _____

  hours: _____

- ❑ Address_____

  _____

  _____

Fees:

- ❑ Day Use $ _____
- ❑ Refund policy

  _____

  _____

  _____

Notes:

Name:
City: ## County:
Plan your trip:

History:

Get the Facts
- ❑ Address_____
- _____
- ❑ Phone
- ❑ Best season to visit
- _____
- ❑ Pet Friendly   Y   N
- ❑ Reservations?   Y   N
- date made_____
- ❑ Distance from home
- miles: _____
- hours: _____

Things To Do:
- ❑ ADA availability
- ❑ Public Restrooms
- ❑ Gift Shop
- ❑ Museum
- ❑ Visitor Center
- ❑ Picnic areas
- ❑ Chamber of Commerce

- ❑ Monuments
- ❑ Art Galleries
- ❑ Tours
- ❑ Street Art
- ❑ Natural Areas
- ❑ Living History
- ❑ Cemetery
- ❑ Amphitheater

Places I Want to Visit in the Area:

Restaurants:
Boutiques & Shops:
Monuments:
Museums:

Budget for this trip:

Parking	$
Food	$
Museums	$
Hotel	$
Shopping	$
Total	$

Notes:

Restaurant:

My Experience:

Shopping:

Best Find:

The shop I want to go back to:

Museum:

The coolest thing I learned about this area:

Other:

Name:

City: County:

Plan your trip:

History:

Get the Facts

- ❑ Address_____
- _____
- ❑ Phone
- ❑ Best season to visit
- _____
- ❑ Pet Friendly   Y   N
- ❑ Reservations? Y   N
- date made_____
- ❑ Distance from home
- miles: _____
- hours: _____

Things To Do:

- ❑ ADA availability
- ❑ Public Restrooms
- ❑ Gift Shop
- ❑ Museum
- ❑ Visitor Center
- ❑ Picnic areas
- ❑ Chamber of Commerce
- ❑ Monuments
- ❑ Art Galleries
- ❑ Tours
- ❑ Street Art
- ❑ Natural Areas
- ❑ Living History
- ❑ Cemetery
- ❑ Amphitheater

Places I Want to Visit in the Area:

Restaurants:

Boutiques & Shops:

Monuments:

Museums:

Budget for this trip:

Parking	$
Food	$
Museums	$
Hotel	$
Shopping	$
Total	$

Notes:

Restaurant:

My Experience:

Shopping:

Best Find:

The shop I want to go back to:

Museum:

The coolest thing I learned about this area:

Other:

Name:
City: County:
Plan your trip:

History:

Get the Facts
- ❑ Address_____
  _____
- ❑ Phone
- ❑ Best season to visit
  _____
- ❑ Pet Friendly   Y   N
- ❑ Reservations?   Y   N
  date made_____
- ❑ Distance from home
  miles: _____
  hours: _____

Things To Do:

- ❑ ADA availability
- ❑ Public Restrooms
- ❑ Gift Shop
- ❑ Museum
- ❑ Visitor Center
- ❑ Picnic areas
- ❑ Chamber of Commerce

- ❑ Monuments
- ❑ Art Galleries
- ❑ Tours
- ❑ Street Art
- ❑ Natural Areas
- ❑ Living History
- ❑ Cemetery
- ❑ Amphitheater

Places I Want to Visit in the Area:

Restaurants:
Boutiques & Shops:
Monuments:
Museums:

Budget for this trip:

Parking	$
Food	$
Museums	$
Hotel	$
Shopping	$
Total	$

Notes:

Restaurant:

My Experience:

Shopping:

Best Find:

The shop I want to go back to:

Museum:

The coolest thing I learned about this area:

Other:

INDEX

- Abingdon Historic District..................158
- Accomac Historic District....................62
- Alexandria Historic District..................74
- Barbours Creek Wilderness....................90
- Bear Creek Lake State Park....................14
- Beartown Wilderness.........................151
- Belle Isle State Park........................164
- Breaks Interstate State Park................120
- Bremo Historic District......................40
- Brush Mountain East Wilderness............149
- Brush Mountain Wilderness..................148
- Caledon State Park..........................162
- Cave Mountain Lake Rec. Area................94
- Charlotte Court House Historic District.....38
- Chippokes Plantation State Park............166
- Clarksville HD& Walking Tour................52
- Claytor Lake State Park.....................130
- Douthat State Park...........................88
- Fairy Stone State Park......................128
- False Cape State Park.......................168
- First Landing State Park....................170
- Fort Myer Historic District..................72
- Garden Mountain Wilderness.................150
- Grayson Highlands State Park................122
- Green Springs Historic District.............50
- High Bridge Trail State Park.................32
- Historic Blackstone..........................54
- Historic Buchanan..........................106
- Historic Downtown Staunton.................104
- Historic Herndon.............................78
- Historic Jamestown..........................176
- Historic New Market.........................112
- Historic Saltville..........................156
- Holliday Lake State Park......................8
- Hungry Mother State Park....................134
- Hunting Camp Creek Wilderness.............152
- Jackson Ward Historic District...............44
- James River Face Wilderness................102
- James River State Park.......................20
- Kimberling Creek Wilderness................144
- Kiptopeke State Park.........................60
- Lake Anna State Park.........................26
- Leesburg Historic District...................82
- Leeslvania State Park........................68
- Lewis Fork Wilderness 124
- Little Dry Run Wilderness...................154
- Little Wilson Creek Wilderness.............138
- Lynchburg Historic District..................36
- Martinsville Historic District................48
- Mason Neck State Park........................70
- Monument Avenue Historic District..........46
- Mountain Lake Wilderness...................145
- Natural Bridge State Park...................101
- Natural Tunnel State Park...................132
- New River Trail State Park..................142
- Occoneechee State Park.......................18
- Peters Mountain Wilderness.................146
- Pocahontas State Park........................12
- Potomac Canal Historic District.............76
- Powhatan State Park..........................22
- Priest Wilderness, The.......................30
- Raccoon Branch Wilderness..................136
- Ramsey's Draft Wilderness....................96
- Rich Hole Wilderness.........................98
- Rough Mountain Wilderness....................97
- Sailor's Creek Battlefield HSP...............33
- Seven Bends State Park......................103
- Shawvers Run Wilderness......................92
- Shenandoah Valley Battlefields National Historic District..........................114
- Shenandoah Wilderness........................29
- Shot Tower State Park.......................153
- Sky Meadows State Park.......................66
- Skyline Drive Historic District.............108
- Smith Mountain Lake State Park..............10
- South Boston Historic Downtown..............42
- Southwest Virginia Museum Historical State Park.......................................140
- Spotsylvania Historic District...............56
- St. Mary's Wilderness.......................100
- Staunton River Battlefield State Park........28
- Staunton River State Park....................16
- Stone Mountain Wilderness...................147
- Three Ridges Wilderness......................31
- Thunder Ridge Wilderness.....................99
- Thunderbird Archaeological District.........116
- Twin Lakes State Park........................24
- University Of Virginia Historic District.....34
- Virginia Military Institute HD...............110
- Virginia Piedmont Heritage Area.............80
- Waterford Historic District..................84
- Westmoreland State Park.....................172
- Widewater State Park.........................71
- Wilderness Road State Park..................126
- York River State Park.......................174

HD: Historic District/Downtown **HSP:** *Historic State Park* **SP:** *State Park*

Notes: